Joyce L. Rapier has been writing since the early 1980's, where she started out writing short stories, ***Whose Life Is It***, for her local paper, The Press-Argus Courier. She published her first three books, ***Windy John's me & Tut***, ***Windy John's Rainbow and the Pot 'O Gold*** and ***Whisper My Name,*** as paperback in the US in November 2002 -2007. Other exciting novels, ***Full Circle*** and ***Red Clay Murders*** followed through 2008 – 2010. Joyce's short stories, ***Hidden Wings*** and ***Messy Kisses*** are inclusions in ***Chicken Soup for the Soul*** and ***Jack and the Mud Pies*** was included in the Literary Cottage anthology, ***My Dog Is My Hero.***

Joyce is married to her high school sweetheart, Dan, and is the mother of three children and eight grandchildren. Now retired, she still maintains presidency and owner of Rapier Inc., a business forms and ad specialty company. Hobbies include gardening, oil painting, writing and a plethora of other personal pleasures. Her personal web site is: www.authorsden.com/joycelrapier where you can read excerpts and peruse original poetry. To purchase books, please refer to www.champagnebooks.com, and www.TigerEyePubs.com.

Joyce L. Rapier

A PICTURE FRAME OF MEMORIES
BOOK I

by
JOYCE L. RAPIER

Edited by Vaughanda Bowie

TigerEye Publications
P.O. Box 6382
Springdale, Arkansas 72766
www.TigerEyePubs.com

Joyce L. Rapier

A Picture Frame of Memories, Book I
Copyright © 2011 by Joyce L. Rapier

All rights reserved. No part of this book may be reproduced or transmitted in any form or by any means without written permission from the author.

ISBN: 9781460942208

Printed in USA

DEDICATION

This book is written in honor of all the memories and to those whose life touched me as a child. Special thanks goes to Editor, Kenneth Fry of the Press-Argus Courier in Van Buren, Arkansas who requested I write a guest column titled, Do You Remember. It has been a rewarding, soul filled venture as I look into the vast corner of my mind to unhinge the memories.

Without my husband, Dan, who recognizes my need to fulfill my writing quest and to all the readers who I meet in stores, those who email me and those who phone, this book would never be written.

Contents

1. Mrs. Sarah Bates..................12
2. Easter Moments..................17
3. Number Please!..................21
4. Bob Burns..................25
5. Downtown Van Buren..................29
4. Stupid Antics..................33
5. Radio Classics..................37
6. Television in the 50's..................41
7. My First Grade Olive Branch..................45
8. Doogies..................48
9. April 21, 1996 Tornado..................52
10. Four-leaf Clover..................56
11. Story of Missionary Pratt..................59
12. Old Cars, Dairy Queen & Moore's Drive-in.....62
13. Strawberry Patches..................66
14. To Wear a Poppy..................69
15. Coal Oil Lanterns..................73
16. Your Father on Father's Day..................77
17. Norman Rockwell Sketch..................80
18. A Favorite Fourth of July..................84
19. The Ice Man..................87
20. Lake Lou Emma..................91
21. Part Two of Lake Lou Emma..................95

A Picture Frame of Memories, Book I

22. Lake Lou Emma Saga......................98
23. WPA..102
24. Going to the Movies.......................106
25. Comic Books..................................110
26. Old Wives Tales.............................114
27. Old Grocery Stores.........................118
28. Teen Town.....................................122
29. Paper Drives..................................126
30. Hand Me Downs............................130
31. Easy Open Packages......................134
32. Lunch Buckets...............................138
33. Best Friends...................................142
34. Salt Pork & Homemade Biscuits...........146
35. Halloween.....................................151
36. Thanksgiving.................................155
37. School Carnivals............................159
38. Christmas Past...............................163
39. Our Charlie Brown Christmas............168
40. New Year......................................172
41. Penny Candy.................................177
42. Tennis Court & Softball Field..............181
43. Valentine's Day..............................186
44. Stilts...190
45. Peanuts & Coke Bottles..................194
46. Victory Gardens............................198
47. Gem Stones & Butter.....................202
48. String Pictures & Yo-Yo's................207

49. Old Sayings & Phrases……………………......211
50. Truant Officers………………………………219
51. St. Patrick's Day……………………………..223
52. Stonehenge & Flintstone Mountain………227
53. Asafoetida……………………………………232
54. Number 10 Wash Tub……………………….236
55. Cardboard Slides…………………………….241
56. Black-eye Peas Tradition…………………….245
57. Danged Old Gremlins……………………….249
58. Calgon, Take Me Away……………………..254
59. Daylight Savings Time……………………….259
60. Van Buren Post Office / Gene Martin……..264
61. Mother's Old Time Remedies………………269
62. Pickett Hill & Crown Hill Cemetery………274
63. Poke Salad…………………………………...279
64. I Dunno………………………………………283
65. Snuff………………………………………….288
66. Sound of the Whistle………………………...293
67. Sulfur Matches……………………………….298
68. The Three Monkey Maxim…………….……303
69. Those Were the Days……………………….307
70. Woolworths & Kress………………………...311
71. Matlock's Grocery Store……………………316
72. Dog Days…………………………………….321
73. Saturday Shopping & Triangle……………325
74. Country Living and Dirt Roads…………...330

A PICTURE FRAME OF MEMORIES

BOOK I

Joyce L. Rapier

PREFACE

Where would we be without memories? Some memories are beautiful but others, sad. It is those memories sustaining us as we go forward with our lives. Reminiscing gives us food for thought to embrace those persons past and present, times changing whether we want them to or not and they forge a way for our well being.

Memories are therapeutic. They make us laugh, cry or feel melancholy and sometimes make us wish we could go back and change things that happen. However, we cannot go back in time to erase, shift or shuffle our lives as a memory waits for no one. It is what we do with these memories, good or bad, ugly or beautiful that counts. A lot of us go through life without thinking of the past and why it is important. Our lives hinge on those coming before us as they mark a time and place in our lives.

Many things can trigger memories…a scent floating on the breeze, walking through tall grasses, hearing someone laugh, pictures, and collected objects. The mind is so vast it can store the minutest vision and unleash it in tremendous volumes. For me, memories are a lasting tribute and flood me with love, tenderness and overwhelming sadness. It is what I do with those memories that make them special.

This book is written with love and sincerity. Everyone I have met in my life has touched me in some way whether it was with a smile, through encouragement or joining me as I traveled the tenure of my childhood. It is my desire that all of you reading this book will take the time to write down the memories locked away in your mind and heart. Without you giving your time
to tell your story, those things dear to you will be lost forever. Time is wasting as time does not wait for man. The only thing that

lives forever are rocks but memories can live through infinity if they are written down and shared with those to come.

To all of you who graciously gave permission to include your names / private businesses in this book, thank you. I do hope you enjoy reading my book and as always…my love to you and thanks for the memories.

MRS. SARAH BATES

While reading the obituary of Mrs. Sarah Bates, a very talented piano forte teacher and wonderful person, I began walking down memory lane as I remembered her lovely smile when she would stop and speak to me. The sparkle in her eyes competed with her dark wavy hair and petite stature. Back in the early 50's when I was a student at Sophia Meyer Elementary School, my normal afternoon walk toward home would take me past Bates' Hardware Store, various main street stores and grand antebellum houses on 7th Street and Broadway.

Going to school, my first obstacle was Swift and Company, a chicken pot pie manufacturer at Knox and Lafayette Street. The north side of the vast building was blistering cold in the winter and hotter than heck in the spring and summer, but at least there was a side walk. It bubbled in spots with cracks and crevices but it was better than nothing, except when it was deluged with rain. Then you could not be certain if it would devour you with its sharp concrete barbs or bury you in mud. The sidewalk took on a persona of its own and seemed to be alive and well - just waiting for its next victim.

Walking under the Frisco train overpass on 7th Street had its menacing grip on me. I was not certain if the train would come barreling from the tracks at break neck speed, the overpass would fall atop me, or the grease and oil would spatter me with smelly gunk. Any way you slice it; I had to go under the blasted thing because I sure as heck didn't want to go over it. It appeared to be a monster of gaping wood teeth.

On the corner of 7th and Main was Citizens Bank with its ornate, double entry doors. Just down the way, between 6th and 7th Street, The Palace Drug Store was one of my favorite places. On occasion, while on my way to school, I would dilly dally around and peer through the windows taking in all the wonders of feminine perfumes. Delicate aromas of Chanel #5 or Coty's Emeraude colognes, wafting through the air, tempted this child to take in all the delightful breath of air I could muster. It had to be heaven because nothing could come close to the scents. Mr. Willis Campbell, the proprietor and smiling gentle soul, always waved at me knowing I would enjoy the pleasures as they chased me forward toward school.

Passing the post office, I knew my path would take me near a Magnolia lined, grand house–a house I was told held a laboratory to dissect young children. Needless to say, my footsteps quickly turned into a downright lope! However, another large, white, two story house glared at me, and my heart leapt into my mouth. It was Ocker Funeral Home, situated on the corner of 7th and Broadway and dictated where my feet would trod. I had no choice. Walk past the scary, monumental place with the black hearse's headlights glaring at me, or turn around and find myself in front of the kid eating house. It was a no win situation. I closed my eyes, darted across the busy Broadway Street, and ran the rest of the way to school. I was safe at last–that is, until the next day and the process would begin again. I don't know how I ever managed to get to school or back home because the routes I had to travel held imaginable, heart pounding, gasping-for-air fears.

Deciding to venture in another direction to go home from school was not too smart. Passing by the dilapidated shanties with its comic book array and often times a stench from mustiness, didn't appease me in the safety mode. Some of the old men, running the stores–if you could call them stores–were not the safest place in the world to be because of the terrifying things I heard about those places. I learned to pinch my nose shut, pretend the old men didn't exist and run like hell. When I was small my feet never touched the ground because I was too busy flying past spooky things.

Going down Main Street, passing Tyler's Five & Dime, Dunn's Shoe Store, Bates' Hardware Store, Skinner's Drug Store, W.B. Smith Dry Goods Store, and waving to people from those delightful places, my next contact was in front of a bank. Now, in this six year old child's mind, the sidewalk was for everyone. Not so, according to one particular man. Every afternoon, like a clock work mouse, the man running the bank would come out and tell us kids to walk across the street and stay away from the bank. Once he had the audacity to grab me by the nape of the neck and I kicked his shin so hard he hobbled on one leg. I swear I could hear his teeth rattle and it was the last time he told me to do anything. Perhaps the fear from all the other menacing places shoved me into a power zone because after the episode, none of the harbingers of doom scared me. It was a piece of cake!

On occasion, I would save pennies from my "morning milk break" at school and shove them inside my shoe. When I had enough pennies, my after school feast would be a giant red apple from Buster Brown's Market, situated at the bottom of Log Town Hill and Knox Street. Shoving the straps of my old, black and red, zippered back pack (yes, we had those sorts of things and I hated it) around my neck; the red apple succumbed to nothing but an apple core. Every other day, my shoes were emptied and the pennies were plopped into Buster's hands. I do miss those "hold 'em with two hands" sweet, delicious, colossal red apples, but I don't miss the indentations of Abraham Lincoln's face on the soles of my feet.

Those days are gone and so are the fears seen by blue eyes of a child. No more antebellum houses with giant Magnolia trees, no cobblestone Main Street where you stub your toes on a jutting brick, no Tyler's Five and Dime, no Dunn's Shoe Store where you could buy refurbished cowboy boots for a quarter, no Bates' Hardware Store (if he didn't have it, you didn't need it), no Skinner's Drug Store, no W.B. Smith Dry Goods Store, no People's Bank, no Palace Drug store, no comic book strip shanties, no Buster Brown's Market, and alas, no Swift and Company on Lafayette Street where I walked everyday to and from school. So many different stores, in the time and place of yesteryear, aligned Main Street proper and it is sad to know they will never be again. It is a part of the past, a delicate piece of history in Van Buren's growing prosperity.

Those places and most of the people who ran them and many more of the once proud mom and pop shops are gone, replaced in part by this person's memory and the smiles touching her.

EASTER MEMORIES

Close your eyes for a few minutes and reflect. Felt good, didn't it? I grew up on Henry Street; better known as part of the "holler." Time stood still in the mind of this little girl as the tick-tock seemed to creep along, and my security, unlike it is today was never in jeopardy. We didn't lock our doors because our neighbors were like an extended family. We didn't have doorbells to announce our presence, but screen doors making it accessible for a quick, "Yoo-hoo." If one person hurt, someone was always there to lend a helping hand. If someone needed something, we gave it willingly with no questions asked. It was perfection, at best.

My part of the world was glorious and childhood memories take me to heights unrivaled. Although we had dirt roads in our neighborhood, the sometimes, quite bumpy, dusty road gave way to exquisite sites. As Robins chirped their arrival, the aroma of daffodils, hyacinths and Bradford pear trees in bloom signaled the season's change, excitably proclaiming Easter would be upon us.

The week before Easter was a prelude to many adventures. If money was available, Hays and Graham's, an up-scale women's clothing store or W.B. Smith Dry Goods store enticed mother in search of the perfect dresses for my sister and me. She wanted me, unfortunately, to have the no-nonsense type of dress I could wear to school (the big, plaid, yucky kind you could have an epic tic-tac-toe game inside the squares) but I, being the mulish, second child of the family, wanted frilly, feminine, pastel attire. However, mother was boss and knew this child, who liked to climb trees, needed something made out of tent material. What she said won and my protests fell on deaf ears. She was my mother and to defy her was a big no, no! To be quite frank, kids didn't defy parents back then, or at least this child didn't. Doing so would mean I would have to go find my own willow tree branch, if you get my drift.

Shoes to match came next. Saddle oxfords, the shoes I tried to kill with a hammer, rocks or anything handy, came in second to the "throw me to the wolves" saga. Not to sound ungrateful, but I hated those gun boats because it meant I would have to wear them in the fall ... if my feet didn't grow. I measured my feet every day, and hoped my toes would curl up inside the steel coated, brown and black or black and white, hideous clod hoppers. Those cockeyed shoes was made of one inch thick leather, and the soles could be slicker than banana peels. One slip of the foot and you were gone, doing the splits and other antics.

Surprise! Mother, on this special Easter, bought the most glamorous yellow frilled dress I ever saw, wide brimmed white hat with yellow ribbon, and black patent shoes to match the ensemble. I was in heaven but didn't know the price she had to pay. I was oblivious to the cost of things but hugged her neck. She cried.

Now, I know there is no Easter Bunny and I knew it as a child, but my imaginations ran rampant. Visions of a giant, white rabbit with large pink ears, placing a basket of eggs on my front porch excited me to no end. It was a thrilling time then, as it is now for little children. I couldn't grasp how a giant rabbit, given its authority on what I liked or where I lived, could find my Easter egg basket secreted in the attic. I crawled up in the attic and hid my basket under dad's gun cleaning kit to see if it would magically appear. Voila, incomprehensible as it seemed, the mysterious rabbit found it, filled it with colored eggs and plopped it on the door stoop.

Easter eggs, dyed purple, yellow, red, and green evokes a precious time for me because it enamored the soul knowing it was time to hunt the oval treasures. Deliberate growth of un-mowed grass (actually weeds) determined how far into the overgrowth I would venture in search of the elusive, hardboiled, sometimes cracked, sulfur laden colored jewels. Sometimes the neighborhood kids would be home and we would swing the baskets of eggs over our heads to see how many would stay inside the green artificial grass. Sometimes, if we were lucky, the eggs would stay intact and off to the wide open field we would trod, placing the eggs in hiding places and yell, "If you don't find one, you will have to eat all of the eggs we find." Our eyes turned a shade of puce green and our lips curled downward with the horrid thought. As it happened, we were sicker than junk yard dogs downing six dozen eggs making the whiff surrounding us tantamount to one of the pungent outhouses.

Afterward, on this glorious Easter Day, we would lay on an old, homemade, patchwork quilt focusing on the firmament. Dare I say this? Inside the clouds, the perfect, white puffy clouds dancing overhead, was the giant, white, beautiful, pink eared Easter rabbit carrying my Easter basket.

Close your eyes ... do you remember?

NUMBER PLEASE!

Do you have your cup of coffee? If you do, go turn off your cell phones, and travel back with me to...

"Number please."

"Operator, will you get me number 711W?"

The reply we always heard was. "Just one minute, please."

What seemed to be an eternity to an impatient wait only took several seconds, and then the other person would say, "Hello?" You had reached your party.

Our old black wall phone didn't have a dial, but a mere receiver and cradle you whacked with your hand to get the attention of the operator. Jiggling the cradle indicated you wanted to phone out to talk to another person. It wasn't like it is today with a nine digit number, instant dial, computer generated, caller ID, or palm messaging. You were given a two, three or four number digit with a single letter attached. The letter indicated "party line." You waited till it was your turn to be on the line but once you were on the line; you could talk your heart's content. Maybe you could, maybe you couldn't, especially if an emergency arose, or someone yelled a static retort, "Get off the line, you phone hog. It's my turn!" Believe it or not, not everyone had a phone, and neighbors would ask to "use or borrow" the phone. Everyone said yes, because in this era a phone was considered a luxury, and we did our part to help our neighbors.

It amazed this little girl how anyone could talk through an ugly hole-filled receiver, and be able at the same time, to hear words flowing across a wire attached to a house as it echoed through the other end of the phone to your ear. It was truly astonishing my conversation could be heard by an operator sitting halfway across town.

Yeah, she could hear it, and so could the "party line" attached to our number. To say "party line" meant another resident, somewhere in the neighborhood or across town, was given access to the same line although their telephone number was different. It wasn't uncommon to lift the receiver and hear someone shouting or giving a few choice words to the intended target. Sometimes they would whisper, thinking the conversation couldn't be heard, but it was ... oh yes, it was! No wonder everyone knew what the rest of the world was doing, what they were having for supper, who had a rip roaring fight, or who was going to go on vacation.

I wasn't allowed to use the phone unless it was an absolute emergency as it wasn't a toy but a necessity. Did I hear an overheard word or two? You bet I did because I was one of the defiant "don't tell me I can't do something" little brats, and actually wanted to take the phone apart to see how it worked. I did screw off the ear piece and punched a few of the wires trying to see where the operator was and how she knew what to do. Mother never had to spank me. All she had to do was tell me to go pull a willow branch off the tree. Blast those trees! I pulled so many limbs off the tree; it was hard to reach them. I was glad when the tree died a natural death.

Since the phone was off limits, the next best thing was a long string with tin cans on each end. Shirley Titsworth Brewer, her brothers, and a friend who lived on Elm Street just off Arkansas Street, and I would gather up a lot of string and cans and make our own telephones.

Careful to punch a small hole in the bottom of the can so the string wouldn't pop out, we strung the string, tied a large knot and paced the distance between houses. We needed lots of string, but not to worry, everyone had a ball of old "saved" string and it did the trick. Never mind the wadded up knots in the string, if we couldn't yank them out, we'd talk over them.

In order to hear what the other kid was saying, the string had to be taut. I don't mean wimpy taut, I mean stiffer than a two by four. Halfway through a muffled, "Can you hear me?" the string would break and we would stop. It appeared the "party line" for the boys was deliberately snapped (they were ornery as cockeyed mules) and Shirley and I were the ones having to run check on downed string. Doing our repairs, we would resume our "single" conversation. Having a talk with oneself, pretending to hear what the other person said got boring. The only thing I managed to get out of the ordeal was a sore, green-bean can drippy ear with a large red ring around my cheek, and devilish blue eyes wanting to do bodily harm to the boys.

Getting fed up with tying knots and smelling the residue from the can, one quick flip of the wrist and the cans were history, back to the cistern from where they came. What did we do?

You guessed it!

"Number please."

BOB BURNS

Top off your coffee, and come sit with me for a while. Rather have latte? Go ahead, I'll wait. We can enjoy this together.

Do you remember Bob Burns? No, I'm not talking about the drummer for Lynyrd Skynyrd. I am talking about Van Buren's own, Bob Burns, better known as "Bazooka Burns" and the "Arkansas Traveler," and inventor of the Bazooka. Born in 1890, his birth name was Robin Burn and he served in WWI as a Marine Sergeant and master rifleman. He was a comedian, actor, and noted for wacky stories about hillbillies. Although I did not know him personally, my dad told me of his inane ability to take the doldrums out of a burdened soul. Bob Burns was also a character whose persona enabled WWII soldiers to have a piece of the "down home, beans and cornbread stories" transmitted by the Armed Forces Radio Broadcast, while our soldiers were fighting on foreign soil. Bob Burns Theater held his moniker for many years until it was changed to The King Opera House. Burns' tales and jokes lifted the weary, giving them a taste of the "good times"; something a lot of us have forgotten.

His home place is on the north corner of 9th and Jefferson Streets, one block north of Sophia Meyer Elementary School. Many times, just to be nosy, I would venture in its direction. Back in the 1950's, the house was grand but not pretentious. Circa 1885, it didn't have massive columns or anything fancy. It reflected Bob Burns, a down home southern boy. I didn't even know Bob Burns had lived there, but relished in its perch upon the hill. It gave off vibes of "look at me" I am something special. It was special, but how many of us even look at it now? Would we recognize it, and understand all it has to offer? Probably not, because historical things sometimes have a way of disappearing, right before our eyes. It is a part of Van Buren's history, but more than that, it is a part of us, a part we take for granted.

In 1905, he invented the Bazooka, one of the silliest musical instruments to ever come down the pike but also, even more important, it's known for being dubbed a rocket launcher used by American Forces to fight the insidious German tanks. If you think about the word Bazooka, you will probably think of a military gun.

The actual prototype, a contraption made out of a whiskey funnel and two gas pipes, was much larger than the ones I "thought" were sold in Tyler's or Sterling's Five and Dime Stores. What we purchased was maybe four or five inches long but could be held by the palm of a child. It was easy to hold but hard on the lips. The ones we could buy were made out of tin or plastic and looked somewhat like an every day, ordinary, partly squashed kitchen funnel with a rosette on top. It was narrow on one end where you pursed your lips with a small hollow tube connecting the opposite end. Right in the middle, a funny looking rosette with squares, was where the sound emitted. There were no keys to play, no slide like there is on a Trombone or sticks to give it a good whack.

The first time I blew on my "Bazooka," no sound came out. It made me mad as a hornet because I had plunked down ten cents for the stupid thing and it did nothing! I twirled around and went back inside the store demanding, "This crazy old Bazooka is broke. It ain't good for nuthin'."

The saleslady just about fell on the floor laughing, and I became more indignant. I was so mad; I think my blue eyes must have turned a shade of black. I might have been only six years old, but I knew when I had been had. "I'm tellin' you, it won't work and I want my money back. I'll go buy an apple because at least it will make a crunchin' sound."

She stared at me, my stanch with hands on hips defying her to keep my money. "Blondie," she giggled. "Do you know how to sing?"

"What's that got to do with that crazy, old Bazooka not makin' music?"

Tears were rolling down her cheeks and she couldn't contain her laughter. Taking me by the hand she led me to the register. "It's not a Bazooka. It's a Kazoo. Stand right there and let me show you how to play it." Reaching under the counter she took out a Kazoo, put it up to her lips and began humming, Twinkle, Twinkle, Little Star.

"You mean to tell me, that thing ain't a Bazooka, and I gotta hum to make it work? What good is that old thing if I have to hum? I can hum without it."

Reluctantly, I walked out of the store with the old tin Kazoo, put it up to my lips and began humming. After a few minutes my lips hurt, my nose began itching and my ears roared.

I put the Kazoo in my pocket, and never bought another one. No, I didn't have a piece of history in my possession, and I never saw an actual Bazooka. We, on the other hand, do have a piece of history to remember and enjoy. It is the Bob Burns house.

Robin Burn, (Bob Burns) 1890-1956

DOWNTOWN VAN BUREN

Coffee, anyone?

How many of you remember down town Van Buren? Are you cocking your head right now and thinking, "That's a redundant question?" Some of you might say, "Sure, I'm there almost every day." Are you, or do you, like me, zip through town without actually looking at the buildings? Could you describe it to someone or would you say it is a quaint little burg?

Visualize living in 1836 when our town was wilderness, the river, a handful of businesses, and a few families making up the area. Did you know two men; David Thompson and John Drennen purchased the area for $11,000.00 and it was incorporated in 1842 and reincorporated in 1845? Questions make my imagination go on a journey to the wild side as I peer through windows of the past. Drastic living conditions rife with dangerous confrontations must have been harrowing. Knowing these things, I stop and look around realizing it took many man hours of hard labor to erect our town. Does it not justify all of us to stop and look at its history and pay homage to its founders?

Have you looked at the capitals (columns or pillars), ogees, brick dental work neatly laid so many years ago, or entryways? How many of them have ironwork stairs leading upward to a veranda? How many of them have been modernized with a false façade? How many of them have a basement? Do any of them have awnings supported by ornate black metal posts? Some windows have elaborate wrought iron surrounds; others are plain. Iron mesh ventilation captures most of the buildings. How many wooden kegs can you count on the sidewalk of downtown Van Buren during the spring and summer as the beautiful flowers waft their wonders?

Do you know how many chimneys and dormers are on top of the Frisco Depot, or how many stores have black stars on the west side of their building? Some stars are red and can be seen on various areas of many buildings. How many of the buildings have a spire perched on top, and have you seen the eagle crest facing north at the corner of 6th and Main, indicating Anheuser Busch Ice House, circa 1892, once graced the old store? An Anheuser Busch sign is printed on the west exterior of the building.

Rosettes and corbels adorn the building at 610 Main, and large letters indicate Edmonson 1895. I wonder what was sold, and was Edmonson a family oriented establishment. Right next door, 612 Main has Boston Store 1896 in big bold letters. It had to be an upscale store as the name evokes grandeur, such as it was in Fort Smith.

A very large white sign is on the west side of 631 Main. Its name, Citizens Bank 1886, is etched in stone on the south façade. Right next door at 633 Main used to be Crawford County Bank. These elegant buildings held the future of Van Buren and helped to make the town grow at a rapid rate.

Look up at 711 Main and see F&AM & KD with symbols adorning the brickwork. F&AM stands for Free and Accepted Masons. However, I have no clue what KD represents. Right next door, caduceus frames the upper exterior of the building. Going further up Main Street at 812 (part of this is the Cottage Café), and 814, have you noticed the round porticos on the buildings, or the mysterious, arched brick entryway adjoining them. It was an ominous feeling to walk through the entryway to visit a doctor who once practiced medicine on the second floor.

    The County Courthouse is a beautiful building. Have you noticed how many benches there are for patrons or balconies adorning the north and east? Were you privy to three entryways to the main building before it was changed to two? Yes, there were three - two on the east (one of them is now a window) and one on the north. The county jail used to be on the south side, and bars and prisoners were visible to anyone going in the area. What about the old Albert Pike School House sitting on the courthouse lawn? Are you aware Albert Pike was a poet and lawyer and taught school in 1882, and then became Editor of the Advocate in Little Rock, Arkansas? Have you read the tributes on the monuments?

    The reason I am asking these questions is do you really see the town? It once was a beehive of activity supporting many families, and supplying citizens with needed products. It was the "hub" of our town, unlike it is today, with one stop shopping and mall venues. Everything a person needed was found in downtown Van Buren. Meat markets, drug stores, dress shops, hardwares, banks, bakeries, cafés, dry-goods, photography, theater, and everything else to sustain our lives. People visited on a regular basis and knew one another by a first name.

Unfortunately, times change and so do all of us. For most people, a town is where you reside, a zip code. Sure, the buildings of our town still stand, but the only constant is a shell, the façade of those lives coming before us, and the price they paid to build the lovely, old town of Van Buren.

STUPID ANTICS

I'm comfy, are you? Take a deep breath and fly with me.

My mother, Lucille Brannam, was as tolerant as Job when it came to my sister and me, and I believe it was how I managed to survive puberty. Without her I would have been long gone at the age of six. We had a wire fence around our yard, not to keep anyone out, but to keep me in. Numerous occasions, I would sneak off just to hear my name being called in a very irate tone. Not from my mother, mind you, but my sister! The only place I ventured was to my grandmother's, two houses north, and it pained me to hear my name being called every few minutes.

My sister, Hazel, was the most gorgeous person I ever laid eyes on, and to this day, I wonder if she realizes how many times I stared at her. She had flowing, long, dark brown hair, olive skin, and eyes as black as coal. Her eyebrows arched gracefully and her lashes fluttered each time she batted an eyelid. She was the spitting image of my mother and everyone knew she was my mother's daughter. I never knew how my sister stayed so clean and pristine. Maybe it was because she liked rolling her hair in Bobbi pins, perusing the Sears Roebuck catalog, singing with our cousin, Billie Dean Harmon Rogoff, and fireflies.

Along comes this offshoot! I had whitish blonde, baby fine hair. When it was wet, I looked like I was bald, and all you could see were two blue eyes peering through non-existent eyelashes and no eyebrows to ward off evil. Yeah, they were there but you couldn't see them. I looked as though I was erased because of my fair complexion. I sunburned, she didn't. My image and penchant for rotten little escapades reflected my dad. I liked grasshoppers, mud pies and climbing anything, especially trees. I inherited well.

On washday, mother would haul out the old wringer washing machine, an ugly contraption hell-bent for leather to swallow up this kid. I loved to smell the lye soap, and watch it swish around in the large metal barrel as the blades ka-chugged the clothes. When it came to wringing them out in the old rollers above the washer, this kid was gone! One little set-to with the arm eating rollers, yanking me between the blades was enough to know it didn't like me. I gave it a wide berth. This was the opportune time to do what I liked to do. I could sneak out and swing on the clothesline before my sister and mother could stop me. Why? Because my sister had to help mother hold the wet clothes to keep them from falling on the floor. It took four hands to do the job, and lucky me, I was too small.

Out the basement door I flew, straight for the clothes line. Our clothes line ran at least fifty feet, north to south, with four metal wires strung between two, giant wood "T" posts. Regardless of how many times I was told to stop swinging on the wires and using them as a trapeze, it had a mysterious hold on me. It was a blast and I pretended I was in the circus. On this particular day, nothing went right. One perfect swing of my legs, and I was dangling downward with my head to the ground swinging to and fro pretending to be on a high wire. All of a sudden, my lights went out. All I remember is mother and Hazel standing over me with a basket of wet clothes and nowhere to hang them. With the weight of my legs, both "T" posts ripped out of the ground sending dirt in all direction and flew overhead, while the wire laid there in a mangled heap. I lay there with a wad of dirt in my mouth and grass between my teeth. When I came to my senses, I saw mother and Hazel standing over me.

Mother sat down on the ground and said, "Oh my Lord. What will I do with all these wet clothes?"

Hazel, in her calmest voice, stated. "Mother, if I were you, I'd just kill her! Please don't ever have another baby because it would be like her. I tried to tell you she was going to jerk it out of the ground." Then she looked at me with those black eyes emitting daggers and proclaimed. "You're gonna get it when daddy comes home."

Did I feel bad? Yes and no. I was sorry for bringing down the clothes line, but there was a solution. I picked up the clothes and draped them across the old wire fence. At least the fence, whose only aim in my life was to keep me in check, came to my rescue.

Was I in hot water with my dad? No, because he knew if I didn't tear it down the weather would. Being the "jack of all trades," Dad welded steel posts making heavy duty T's, buried them five feet in the ground, used large eye hooks to string the four wires between the steel posts, and mother never had to use a wood prop again. The wires were so taut they pinged if you plucked them.

Did I swing on the wires again? "She'd fly through the air with the greatest of ease, this daring young Joyce on the flying trapeze."

RADIO CLASSICS

Grab a blanket, a cup of hot chocolate and shiver with me...

Shh. Don't anyone make a sound. BAMB! All of a sudden, you hear a loud squawk. It jerks the hair upright and cold chills shiver up your spine, as a twist of the knob finds the proper channel on the old, arch shaped, Bakelite or wood tone radio. Then a hushed breath escapes into the atmosphere, and you think, perhaps, it won't be as scary as the last time. It's quiet and dark in the house as everyone huddles together anticipating the organ music's eerie, menacing, screeching door to plummet them inside "Inner Sanctum Mysteries" and its story of mystery and intrigue. Tales of murder, insane asylum bludgeoning, escaped convicts, and apparitions lurked through the tones of a raspy throated story teller, as he hooked you with the barb of a sinister plot and took you on a roller coaster ride of chilling, epic tales. It scared the beejeebers out of me!

It was radio drama ... drama touching senses of sight, hearing, taste, touch and smell. We couldn't see the radio stars, but through their magnificent portrayal, they managed to entertain listeners. All across the United States, or those places who could tune in and hear through all static popping interference, folks couldn't wait for the next episode. It was majestic.

Do you remember Fibber McGee and Molly, Gildersleeve, and its characters? Hilarious antics pulled you into the show while parts of their script made you cry, laugh, gasp, and think. Many miles away in a small radio station, these delightful stars transformed our lives through a microphone. It was like they were sitting in your house conversing with you on a one to one basis.

Gun Smoke, radio's last drama, made you feel as though you were sitting in Dodge City, Kansas fighting the bad guys with Matt Dillon (James Arness), Chester (Dennis Weaver), Miss Kitty (Amanda Blake), and Doc (Milburn Stone). You could hear the ricochet of bullets shear through the radio and smell the gun powder. Thundering hooves plowed down 1872 - 1885 roads making you cough with the onslaught of dust as it filtered through the air. It was powerful. The senses were used and you felt good knowing Matt Dillon wore the white hat. You didn't need to see the white hat ... it was in your mind.

Dragnet, Jack Webb's original radio drama 1949 - 1959, brought terrifying scenes to your living room. The opening line on radio by George Fenneman, "The story you are about to hear is true, only the names have been changed to protect the innocent," placed you square dab in the middle of police procedures. Hearing tires squealing, gun shots and screams made your heart palpitate at a rapid rate. Jack Webb, (Joe Friday), was a master in making true, live episodes so real; you could feel his footsteps approach as a door slammed and he began his narrative. "Wednesday, December 12. It was cold in Los Angeles. We were working the day shift...." Each of his comments was precise, to the point, and always ended with, "My name's Friday."

Ted Mack and the Original Amateur Hour brought new singing artists to the forefront. Our hearing was delighted even though some contestants sang a tad off key. Object is you heard it. Lum and Abner, Mt. Ida's zany duo, was down home originals whose penchant for country talking matched our speech to a "T." We identified with those characters. Johnny Dollar, The Shadow, and Bobby Benson and the B-Bar-B Riders were other shows we "watched" on radio.

Was it a sign of times in grander things to come as radio shows were pushed from the limelight, or did America grow weary of what they thought they couldn't see? Television was gradually pushing its way forward, demanding its share of the glory by "showing" us what we needed to see. Everything is relative, as once again, progress lunges forward making access to a new generation.

Back when, people used their imagination to its fullest. They didn't have to see something to know what was happening, it was in vivid color, dancing like 3D pixels across their mind. If a woman was told she had ladders up her stockings, she didn't have to look at it, she knew what they were. If a man was told he had a five o'clock shadow, he didn't have to look in a mirror to know he needed a shave. We've been given so much freedom to forget about an imagination, it's hard to digress in search of what we had. Sure, we've come a long way but at what price?

All of these shows are gone now, but for some of us, aren't forgotten. Now, it's a reflection, a past era of gentleness, a quiet repose, a time to make the mind think and use its resourcefulness, and reflect to what it was like to "watch" shows on radio.

Shh! It's time to take back what we've given away ... our precious resources touch, smell, hearing, taste and sight. It's called an imagination.

TELEVISION IN THE 50'S

Instead of coffee, how about a glass of ginger ale and a platter of liver patties (don't frown!) I assure you, the liver patties are delectable and I am proud to say I still have mother's original recipe. They go good with this story. This is how they are made. Buy a pound of liver or carton of chicken livers. Wash and pat dry. Using a meat grinder, pulverize each piece of liver. Place in a colander to drain any excess liquid. Set aside. After you have washed the meat grinder, peal one small onion and grind it as you did the meat. Drain and set aside. When the liver and onions are drained, mix together. Mash several saltine crackers (our crackers came four to a square but are now single crackers). Do not salt the meat and onions as the salt in the crackers will do the trick. You can add black pepper or cayenne flakes if you like the hot flavor. Mix the saltines with the liver and onions as the binding ingredient. Make small balls and then flatten and roll or pat more saltines to the exterior of the patties. Deep fry or pan fry the patties till done. Let the patties drain on paper towels or on a metal rack. They are delicious. Now, back to my story!

Exit radio watching, enter TV. When did you get your first television set? Was it a mammoth Zenith or an Admiral? The reason I ask is because TV and snacks go hand in hand. Our snacks included a large glass of ice cold ginger ale and liver patties as we enjoyed the transition from radio watching to sitting in front of a television set. Yes, I was part of the last generation of radio watching and a first generation to see action at its best.

My first viewing of a television program was at the Green's house on Arkansas Street. It was dark outside as my family walked up the dirt road and my mind was focused on seeing people come alive, something I heard for a week. We enjoyed going to the Green's house until daddy decided to buy a TV, and then it was our turn to invite people to our house. Our TV was a Zenith, and as the word zenith means overhead or above the horizon, we were looking into the horizon of a fast paced, soon to be world, but didn't realize how fast it would spin.

Watching the test pattern was as boring and irritating as listening to a dripping faucet. There had to be more to life than sitting there watching a box with a black and white, stationary picture and hearing small talk from the adults. Then it happened! It transformed right before my eyes.

I don't remember the preface to the show, commercials or such, but seeing Brian Donlevy, a broad shouldered, neatly attired, mustached man in Dangerous Assignment (1952), kept me glued to the somewhat square, thick, pop bottle screen TV set. Espionage was the theme. In the foggy shipyard, a very large dagger whizzes past Steve Mitchell's face while his behavior is nonchalant. He exhales cigarette smoke and flicks ashes as he knows no fear; he has seen it all, murder, theft and many dangerous assignments. I was hooked and couldn't wait for the next episode. It was magical to know a person could be in your house, and when you got tired of them you could flip it off.

Dragnet (1951-1959), starring Jack Webb as Joe Friday and his cohorts, continued from the radio shows to classic television programming. Seeing the sweaty fist, grasping a heavy hammer while pounding an anvil to the beat of "dum-de-dum-dum ... dum-de-dum-dum-DUM!" you knew immediately it was the famous Dragnet. There was no long monologue but short sentences, usually with one or two words. It was always, "Yes, Ma'am, No, Ma'am, or Just the facts, Ma'am, just the facts." Realism brought the passé radio show to life on the silver screen.

Kent Taylor, Boston Blackie (1951-1953), was another detective show. He was suave and debonair with a wily disposition. A hat perched atop his jet black hair made you wonder if he was a bon-a-fide detective or the jewel thief in Jack Boyle's original book, Boston Blackie of 1919. The show didn't last long but it was one of my favorites. It had an air of sophistication with intense drama.

Enter the red haired comedian. I Love Lucy, (1951-1957), was the most hysterical comedy I ever watched. Lucille Ball was the ultimate in style, delivery and routine. Always hammering her husband, Ricky (Desi Arnez), to put her on stage with his Cuban band, slam dunked her into hot water. One show left me in stitches. Tired from traveling, they checked into a seedy motel. Almost asleep, a freight train roars past and rocks them out of bed. Fear on Lucy's face almost complimented the red hair that appeared to have been put into an electrical outlet.

Other TV classics: The Perry Como Show, Your Hit Parade, The Jack Benny Show, People Are

Funny, The George Gobel Show, Milton Berle, and so many others brought great pleasures to an era just beginning to emerge in the 20th century. So many of these great people are gone now, but they gave way to bigger and better television shows, mimicked by some but not entirely mastered. TV shows of the 50's were stylistic and pioneered today's viewing.

It's wonderful to look into the past and remember the way it was. However, I must confess, getting up to turn a knob to another channel (not many existed) or turning the volume up or down left a lot to be desired. Today, there are no knobs, no large picture tubes, no giant TV sets (unless its flat screen), waiting for the test pattern to disappear, or turning off the TV when the station went off the air.

Just like everything else we see in our rearview mirror, things of today will dwindle away and be history, and this generation will say, "Do you remember?"

MY FIRST GRADE OLIVE BRANCH

My first grade stomping grounds was Sophia Meyer Elementary School on Broadway. The northeast side of the building housed first grade classes and second progressed in age toward the northwest. As a child got older, the southwest devoured third and fourth, and then the south quad of the building demanded fifth and sixth grade students. Being small, the structure appeared enormous, with its crank out windows and radiators and massive thick walls determined to squelch unruly kids, lurched forward to demand its educational staunch.

I will never forget my first day of school. Dressed in the most awful corduroy slacks held up by gallowses, a yellow and black plaid, button up the back dress to make sure I was covered from head to toe, and those hideous saddle oxfords, I felt like a waif in wait. It was a good thing to wear the corduroy slacks as I dangled with my head toward the ground on the jungle gym. My first grade teacher, Mrs. Dorothy Gregg, was one of the most wonderful women I have ever known. She greeted all of us as we entered the main doors. Directing us to our chairs, she smiled the entire time and soothed those who cried, having just been torn from their mothers' apron strings. She was a small framed woman with a disability but it didn't deter her ability to teach. She wore the sweetest fragrance and it reminded me of daffodils. Neatly attired, with her brown hair coiffed in a bun, she guided all of us with authority. I adored her.

My desk was in the center of the room next to a red haired girl, Linda, (won't tell the last name). Her temperament was as fiery as her natural curly hair. We took one look at each other and knew blistering hell was going to break loose. Putting away our pencils, crayons and wide margined writing paper, Linda dropped her crayons on the floor. I started to help pick up the crayons and without warning my right arm and hand was void of skin. Holy Minerva! Linda's cat like claws, sharper than razor blades, uncoiled from the tips of her fingers and ripped the daylights out of me. The cat fight was on and twenty-five kids were screaming bloody murder. I grabbed her by the hair and pushed her face into the desk while she continued to extract blood from my arm. We were raging battle kin to Patton's push. Right then and there, the teacher separated us, but knew this battle wasn't over. She was right.

The jungle gym was a magnet for all the kids. We gravitated to it like bees to honey and waited our turn for a go at the top bar. It was my turn and I began to scale the octagon shaped rungs but it was short lived. Linda grappled me by my foot and jerked me down to the ground telling me it was her turn. Pulling out some of my ponytail, she shoved it in her pocket. I was mad, downright mad. One way or another, I was going to cure her of slashing me with her claws and pulling out my hair. I remembered mother telling me how she cured her brother of pinching her and I would apply her cunningness toward Linda. It would work, or the both of us would be dead: Linda by head smashing and me with no dermatitis.

After recess, we marched back into class. All sweaty, I sat down at my desk, she at hers. Out of the corner of my eye, I recognized the bright red fingernail polish on my adversary slowly inching its way in my direction. Her hand was now in close proximity and I was determined to engage my defense mechanism. Furtively, I bent over, took off one of my heavy shoes and slammed it as hard as I could. My shoe and her fingernails made contact. No, it didn't break her fingers but it did snap several fingernails into shards.

Our teacher knew what happened but didn't say a word. She pranced over to our desks and told me to put my shoe back on. Reaching into her pocket, she took out a fingernail clipper and proceeded to cut off all of Linda's fingernails and told her she was giving them to me. Yuk!

The next day, much to the teacher's chagrin, she was waiting on both of us. She knew if Linda and I were face to face, daring each other to provoke or instigate battle; she would have to take us both to the principal's office. It didn't happen and she was shocked at our passiveness.

Unbeknownst to our teacher, after school on the day of the fingernail and hair caper, Linda and I made peace. We stared at one another and laughed as we looked like the showdown at OK Corral, she with a goose-egged forehead and I with gouged skin. On the school grounds, she gave me my hair and I gave her the fingernail clippings. Together, we dug a hole and buried them.

It was our olive branch.

DOOGIES

Funny isn't it that marbles or doogies, as we called them way back when, don't show up until it is time for school. On rainy days, I remember sitting in the floor shooting marbles at a tin can or flipping them with my thumb and fore finger. Blast it all, those things would raise a pump knot on the forehead or crack teeth with over exuberant tosses. Not to mention, if you slid barefoot on a passel of them, you might wind up with stone bruised feet or a cracked shin bone. You might wind up spread eagle on the floor wondering why you didn't pick them up off the floor. Like most kids, the brain doesn't kick in with common sense until you turn forty! By then, it's too late, as you can't turn back in time to find what you didn't have.

You could buy a large bag of marbles at the Five & Dime store for ten cents. They looked so pretty in a cubicle mounded up in a pile until a child decided which bag to choose. They came assorted but I always wanted the bag containing red veined Cat's Eye or butterflies. My all time favorite was the red Devil's Eye with a yellow eye center. It was gorgeous. Marbles came in a blue or red mesh bag tied with a ribbon and more often than not, it contained around 100 or more marbles. Bright colored glass marbles, as large as a thumb, rattled inside the bag when shook and scattered like the dickens if you opened them before you got home. Those things rolled down Main Street by the dozens and little feet ran post haste to pick them up off the cobblestone. I never did find all that I lost, and spit and sputtered because my dime reduced to a penny. Somewhere in the confines of the drainage ditch was a clog the size of a car.

Oh, the games you could play with marbles. The kids in my neighborhood drew a circle in the dirt and we took turns seeing who could knock the marbles of their opponent out of the ring. The game was "keepsies" and no one wanted to go home empty handed...especially when you lost some of your favorite marbles.

Sometimes we would dig a small hole (about the size of a nickel) in the ground. The players stood behind a line three or four feet from the hole and we played golf using a long branch from a tree as a club. Most times the branch would break and then we used the stub as a pool cue. It wasn't the easiest thing to do because eyeing the marble toward the hole; we had to lie on our stomachs. Then the marble veered in all directions because of bumpy dirt and pebbles and our elbows gouged the ground. Take it from me we were a mess.

Having a bit of ingenuity, we cut various sized holes in the bottom of a small cardboard box. We numbered some of the holes from five to 100 and cut one larger hole in the center and it was 500. Each of the small holes our marble landed we got those specific scores but if you went inside the large hole, you lost your points plus 500. The losing marbles stayed on the ground until the game ended and then we had to figure out whose marbles were whose. The box usually won and we squabbled as to who would get the chipped marbles. Sometimes it became a raging battle because we swore we didn't play the game unless our marbles were perfect. If we had any smarts, we might have figured out glass marbles crack when hit by another one.

Another game we played was drawing an eight-foot diameter circle. We dug a hole, one foot in circumference, right in the center. Around the hole, we drew additional circles, each larger than the other. Each kid used thirteen solid color marbles laying them two inches from the edge of the hole. If there were three or four players, we had to draw a single color to use. One could use thirteen red or thirteen green and so on. You had to flick the marble with the thumb, as the objective was to stay within the circles and not shoot your own marble into the hole. Whichever thirteenth color marble stayed in the playing field won all the marbles in the hole. Another stupid thing we did with marbles is see which kid could ping them farther into the air with a homemade bean flip. We didn't realize they would come down faster than they went up and hitting the top of the head...hurts! We never shot any of the marbles at anyone for fear of having our rear ends blistered by adult authority. It was bad enough having the head bonked and we didn't need the opposite end of our anatomy hurting too. As we tired of these games, out came the Chinese checkers board. It was a safe game to play.

Lucky for me, daddy collected all kinds of marbles. He let me look at or count them but they were off limit to my games. His were made of pure agate or "aggie." He had some varieties of Indian (mostly black), many steelies and alabaster marbles. Some were deep ruby red stone bloods almost the size of a quarter, solid plaster and tons of regular size marbles. His collection now belongs to me. Tucked away in a safe deposit box are the rare and exotic marbles. As I reflect back on all the games we played, marbles has a place in my heart.

    Marbles were a sign of the times...glass orbs so beautifully designed...down town on the ground you might find one of mine...that I purchased from the Five & Dime.

APRIL 21, 1996 TORNADO

Sunday afternoon was glorious. Old sol was raging down at a ninety degree temperature and the spring flowers were at a harmonious state with nature. What else could be more delightful than digging in terra firma to know the plantings would bring summer repast, or feeling my grandson whose excited, mischievous adventures play tag on the strings of my heart?

It was now four in the afternoon and on the horizon lay an ominous feeling. Thick, dark clouds were gathering at a rapid rate in the west, but the beautiful rays from the sun cast multicolored hues against a backdrop of green trees. It was picturesque, almost like a Monet scene and somewhat tranquil. Soon the clouds disappeared and agreement with the birds and nature filled the air. Nothing could shatter this wonderful state of bliss, or could it?

Later, as our grandson went home from an overnight stay, and the day wore on and night filtered among us, we had no clue of what would transpire or befall our peaceful surroundings. Peace as we knew it would become a nightmare of anguish.

Now, it was dark, extremely dark, unlike the normal nighttime we all can relate. A greenish glow hovered like fingers reaching out to foretell things to come. It was eerie, a fog like state of menacing acts about to be perpetrated on innocent people, without cause but with definite purpose. Rain began to fall, proportioned rain, a quiet rain and lifted the cloud surrounding us. It was soothing and appeared to be nothing more than a gentle sprinkle for eager plants.

Soon, the eerie manipulation returned bringing with it treacherous coiling wind. At points, cool breezes mixed with humid air fought for airspace, trying to exhaust each other with unending power surges. Weather forecasts reverberated with an impending thunderstorm or possible tornado approaching at a rapid rate from the southwest in Pushmataha County in Oklahoma, and for those in its path to take immediate cover. Then, a quiet repose settled bringing with it uneasiness. Rain pelts the earth with a mighty force as winds whip the gale forward. Hail begins to pound the house with enormous thuds, as a low, threatening wall cloud forms like a blanket around the perimeter. Quiet resumes.

It's now around 11:00 p.m., and the power goes off in our house. Fumbling to get out of the bed and searching for my husband, Dan, I walk to the back door. He is standing there watching a tornado bear down toward Mt. Vista. Quickly, he tells me to take cover and runs to the office for important documents, grabs our dog from the garage and meets me inside our center bathroom. We crouch there as the twisting tail from a massive tornado, like a giant scorpion stings the life of its prey, devours and mangles everything in its wake. The sound was that of a thousand horses' hooves, thundering in sync at a rapid rate, in search of lost souls, beckoning to be snatched from the earth. The dark steed of death hovered, waiting, waiting to consume the remains.

Creaks rattle our brick house as shattering windows tear shards of material from drapes, and we hear trees moan and wail as their life is ripped from the sustaining soil, and material from neighboring houses is blown into ours at terrific force. Hearts pounding and with dismay from knowing our once serene lifestyle was thrown into a tumultuous shamble, we regain our composure and embrace. Our lives had been spared. Our panic surges once again as we thought of our children. Without hesitation and not knowing what he might encounter, Dan left the house to make certain our children were safe. He did not know it but they were in route to ours. An hour later, through police roadblocks and debris, the children and Dan came home. Safe in our home, my daughter, Lori, told about having to take refuge under a bridge. She, her husband and son, along with several other people were hinged and hanging on to metal supports to keep from being sucked into the tail of the horrid tornado. Roadblocks were set up and sirens blared. One state trooper was heard saying, "You better bring a lot of body bags, this area is obliterated."

Throughout the night, we had no way of knowing what the neighborhood had endured or what we would view come morning. Fretfully, we slept. Dawn didn't see us awake, the dark, wee morning did, and we were aghast at the devastation. The once majestic oak trees lay hinged to the earth, begging for life. Houses were annihilated and so were the happy lives once occupying them, but one positive thing, no deaths were reported on Mt. Vista or in Van Buren. Sadly, two children in the Fort Smith area were killed when giant trees fell upon their house. It was devastating to know small children would never dance on their lawns or sing, or grow to be adults.

Pain etched the faces of men, women and children as they knew what they worked for all their lives was destroyed in the blink of an eye. Tempers flared where calm composure usually preserved. Disgusting scents wafted through the air from moldy residue within the soil and from fishy, river water deposited in and around the area. Later, as people reviewed their realm, all you could hear was the sound of chainsaws growling at mach speed, spitting and spewing remains of a hundred years growth. Enormous roll off bins could be seen on nearly every street of Mount Vista. As one was filled to capacity, another replaced its spot on the asphalt. Mounds, in thousands of tons, were hauled to the dump and among the debris lay people's lives. Roof rafters, metal garages, out buildings, shingles, warped or mangled toys, window frames and assorted other personal belongings could not be salvaged.

The tornado cut a swath through other areas north of Mount Vista. A fire station was literally ripped from its foundation as were houses and businesses. Nothing was left standing except for the areas people used for refuge. It was as though the mighty tornado deliberately danced across the lives of many, wielding its power to the fullest but resisted the temptation to commit murder. The Van Buren, Arkansas, F-five tornado, having spun many mini tornados around its perimeter, lifted its flogging whip and left scars on its victims.

On this decimate eve, and every time I hear a chain saw, I am reminded of the tornado of April 21, 1996.

Joyce L. Rapier

FOUR-LEAF CLOVER

Think about this for a minute and search your memory. Do you know to what song I am referring when I say it was written by Mort Dixon in 1927 with the tune credited to Harry Woods? It was popularized by Art Mooney in 1948. It was a rather tinny, simple piano rendition, as the early pianos plunked out hollow resonance in an unsophisticated studio or recorded at home. The recorders of 1948 were large, using reel to reel and covered a large space; unlike it is today with technological advances. Every band member or singer attended a recording session and did retakes 'til it was perfect. If you want to record multiple instruments today, they can dub you at a later date or do a voice over, making your appearance unnecessary at the demo.

If you chose this song, you would be correct. When I was small, I sang "Four-leaf Clover" © 1927 not thinking of the meaning or how it was phrased. It was a catchy little tune and easy to memorize, but I didn't realize the petals had meaning or cared. The tune stuck in my head and was impossible to erase because if I sang the song loud enough, surely I would find one of the elusive, so called, lucky four-leaf clovers. Did I actually overlook a four-leaf clover or was I looking over one in desperation to find it or do I have one in my hand looking over its beauty? Does the song have a meaning of an overlooked suitor or are you looking at a person and seeing them in a different light? It's complicated to a degree. Whatever you or I choose to think, the song is classic with its verbiage. It's only eight lines long, repeated over and over with modulations in tone, but for me, it makes a statement. Though it may not have definite hook (what you remember most in current songs), "Four-leaf Clover," as a whole, is complete with a hook, line and tag.

Remember the rosy and sometimes deep hued, crimson clover buds and how erect they stood in the sunshine? Fields were covered with anxious blossoms waiting for bees to pollinate. Then in sadness, they drooped as they scattered tiny seeds to germinate a next season's growth. Clover was everywhere and no one was in a hurry to exterminate them with an old, squeaky, four blade push mower. Kids waited in anticipation to uncover the coveted lucky charm and could be heard screaming, "I found one!" Most of the kids in my neighborhood searched and plowed through the clover and gave it a good whack when nothing turned up positive. Often, one of us could be heard doing a high-pitched wail after a bee sat down on an improper spot.

Patience is virtuous but not without delicate balance ... a balance of kid vs. bees. Then all patience shoots out the door as you vie to see which one can fly or run the fastest. Many times BB guns were aimed at the "you're invading my territory," yellow, poison inflicting, speed demons, but the ball bearing sharpshooters never made contact. Once in a while, those kids owning a tennis racquet would hold the bees to the ground and put their ear close to the profanity spewing bee to see if its "bzzzsst" could be translated. Slap stick comedy unfolded as they ran like the dickens when it escaped through the mesh. As Forrest Gump would say, "Stupid is as stupid does." Our box of chocolate had stupid written all over it in big, bold, red letters.

As I look back, it was wonderful being a child and I delighted immensely in what the world had to offer. A simple, little, perky, honey making clover charmed me knowing it could come back year after year to enthrall dozens of kids with its propensity to make wide eyes search for its creation. In all my searches, I found only one four leaf clover and kept it for years until it disintegrated into a million pieces. I have no idea if it was a lucky four leaf clover or if anything exists as a lucky charm but at the time, I didn't care. It was a four leaf clover, a quirk of nature, a child's find. How simple could life be and why can't it be this way again? Could it be we don't have the patience, time or the desire to be a child again?

I am ready to find a patch of clover, sit in the middle of it, pick my way through the jungle of entwining leaves and sing the words, "I'm looking over a four-leaf clover..." You know the tune but if you don't know the rest of the lyrics, they can be found on the web.

If you see someone in a clover patch near you, it might be me. Listen real close as I will be singing the tune embedded from my childhood, and who knows, you might hear me scream, "I found one!"

STORY OF MISSIONARY PRATT

How many of you have taken the time to write down all the necessary information about your ancestors? If you are like a lot of people, (I'm included), you could say why bother, I'm with my relatives all the time or who needs to know? You do and I will tell you why.

I do know a lot about my family history on my father's side because some of my relatives took the time to list all the names of brothers and sisters, marriages, divorces, and dates of births and deaths. However, did you know when the ancestors are listed; it is only through the male side of the family to carry on the family name? Women who have given birth to multiple children or a single child are not listed in rank through any kind of search engine on the web. The only time a woman's name is listed is to give credit to the father of the child. When she marries and gives birth, it's listed under the spouses' name. Not hers!

Sure, you can request death certificates from a funeral home if you need personal data but it is not always complete. Way back when, sometimes the person giving the information at a death did not know the date a person was born or who their parents were. If a person was an only child, chances are they were apart from their family and were making a life of their own. Most times, people worked so hard they didn't write anything down for reference and it's like they never existed. Family bibles held certain information from those taking the time to write down important information but today, it's not the norm.

The reason I am writing this is because my paternal grandmother's maiden name was Pratt. The minute I read the story about Missionary Parley Parker Pratt (thank you, Kenneth ... great story), I rummaged through all my family tree history, pulled out old pictures to see if there was a resemblance to Mr. Pratt, and emailed my sister. Although my sister knew about the missionary and told me Daddy took her, many years ago, to the grave site where Mr. Pratt was supposedly interred, she wasn't certain if we were related. She said it was possible but her records stopped where mine did.

My grandmother, Della Mae (Pratt) Mahan Brannam Crabtree, was the daughter of May (Russell) Pratt, 4/30/1872-1/9/1948. Her brother's name was Arthur Lee "June" Pratt. She and her brother took the name Mahan when May Russell Pratt married John Dean Mahan, 1/26/1867-7/23/1927 in Cook County Texas. Unfortunately, I will never know about the Pratt name because the Cook County courthouse burned and all the records were destroyed. No where can any of these records be retrieved and doing a search on the internet turns up no listing of my grandmother or her brother.

Missionary Pratt's time on this earth was gone by the time my grandmother was born but Pratt is not a common name. Possibly a relative of Mr. Pratt was my great grandfather. Too bad I will never know this part of my family history and chances are the relatives of Missionary Pratt don't have the information either. A part of my past is lost forever, a piece of knowledge I can't pass to my children. Will I lose any sleep over not knowing? No, because things have a way of working themselves out and perhaps, I don't need to know. I've gone this long without knowing so I will put the newspaper clipping about Missionary Pratt with all my other "passed down" information and let my kids sort through it. Boy, are they going to have a mess to sort through? On the other hand, I am curious. I would be a liar if I said I wasn't. Maybe, just maybe, I will pick up the phone and let my fingers do the walking or email someone in Utah who might have the answer.

    One way or another, whether we like it or not, everyone on this earth is related in some grand pause for thought as humans marry and have children and divorce and die. It's only when we take the time to list parents, siblings, and grandparents that we understand where, why and what we are about in our daily routines.

Joyce L. Rapier

OLD CARS, DAIRY QUEEN AND MOORE'S DRIVE-IN

What kind of car did you have in the late 1950's and 60's? Were you able to work on one when it decided to stall, did you change its oil and filter and how many of you banged out dents with a hammer when a little fender bender caused you grief? Were you one of the teens whose only desire in life was to drive a "soup" Deville and show it off on the Dairy Queen parking lot or Moore's Drive In? Let's take a look in the past to view some of the vintage, four wheel beauties and do a Diamonds, "Come, let's stroll" down to the "hop," where we can think about our youth.

There was the Ford Wagon with its unusual wood grained sides and interior. Roll down windows and am radio was the uptown feature on this massive metal frame with the spare tire employed on the rear of the car. The Ford Skyliner captivated drivers with its partial skylight. Whitewall tires and fenders not quite ready for fins showed off its splendor. No one can forget the Fairlane 500 with fins dancing out at its side or the dual headlights. It was sleek, almost as grandeur as the Fairlane ragtop. Then there was the Edsel sporting the grill in the fashion of a lemon. Every time I use a lemon, a picture of the Edsel pops into my mind. Mustangs became popular in the mid 60's and it was, by far, a teen car. Forget the mom and pop passenger cars, no teen wanted to be seen in one of those.

I suppose the Chevy was most popular with the younger generation. Let's face it, who didn't want a Corvette? The Corvette was the most coveted car, shiny as a new penny and made the heart pound when it approached a stop light. All heads would turn to see who was driving the best designed vehicle and hearing the thundering vroom under its hood. You knew you might as well pack it in as it was too costly. The 1953 Corvette grill reminded me of a shark with its round hood holding it in check as it sped down the road demanding attention. The 1957 Chevy Bel Air was the car to be had and most often it was the chosen car. It was normally a two-toned beauty; dominant color in the front with white pin stripes and fins adorning the rear.

It was not uncommon to hear barking of the tires or listening to someone laying rubber to see whose car was faster. Revving the motor indicated a race was on, especially in front of the old Dairy Queen at 12th and Main Street. Situated on the south side of Main Street, The Dairy Queen was the "hangout" or "drag" for teens in the late 50's. On a normal weekend, cars would be lined up in droves or packed like sardines to get the best "show off my car" spot. Not to mention, but I will, the Dairy Queen had the best malts and sundaes a mouth ever touched. Oh, and who could forget the topped off swirl of the delectable chocolate dipped ice cream cones? We would bounce back and forth from the Dairy Queen to 13th and Main Street's north corner where Moore's Drive-In served up burgers so mouthwatering, you couldn't stop at one burger.

It was as though the Dairy Queen, Moore's Drive-In and Van Buren's own teens invented the movie, "American Graffiti." George Lucas' movie wasn't released till 1973 but for all practical purposes, we lived it before Richard Dreyfuss and Ron Howard made it into the spectacular movie of the year. The movie was a re-run of our lives, played out in living color on the silver screen. Yes, the old black and white police car made its normal appearance wherever the gang got together and sirens screeched through the air whenever a couple of teens decided to out maneuver the wits of the local police force. However, I never heard tale of those pulling the rear axle from under a squad car. Racing was about the only thing the male species did, notwithstanding having their heads stuck inside the hood, or their body under a jacked up car. Axle grease, motor oil and gasoline ($.15 a gallon) is what they thrived on during those fun years.

Visiting the Diary Queen, in a Chevy Coupe or Ford vehicle or one of the other cars of the year, was the highlight of an uneventful, small town week-end. It happened on a regular basis but I am here to tell you, the teens were NOT bad kids. None of them deliberately set out to hurt anyone. Yes, we were loud, as all teenagers are, but respected limitations. Some teens were rough but only on the edges, not to the core. They worked hard for the money they spent and most times the money was used to "soup" up the wheels. They didn't hold out their hand waiting for their parents to dole out money. They got a job ... whatever kind of job they could find and didn't complain. Every one of the teens of the 50's era who still reside in Van Buren is a respectable, viable citizen.

The Chevy and Ford cars of the 50's are considered antique and some of them are moving in glory, proudly displaying their fins in road shows. Gasoline is over the top in price and the "hang outs" are no longer in our midst. The constant is the memories, the teens that made the Dairy Queen and Moore's Drive-In popular places, the cars that made the teens and the drive to push them forward.

Joyce L. Rapier

STRAWBERRY PATCHES

How many of you remember the strawberry patch by Twin Bridges going into Alma?

To the right on highway 64, just past the silver bridge, was the most fabulous place in the world to pick those delectable, mouth watering, ripe, juicy strawberries. The patch belonged to Newt Black, my grandfather-in-law, Val Rapier's cousin. At the time, I didn't know who owned it nor did I know my future husband's grandfather was probably handing me the handy dandy, carry all you can, wood crate. Today, when I pass the area I think lovely thoughts of a time and place I wouldn't trade for the world.

My first experience in picking them was not to my liking because I hated putting on long britches and long sleeved shirts, and I detested the ticks and chiggers I knew would be lurking around just to jump on me. Walking into the patch, we ambled to a small shed somewhere on the north forty, close to the creek. It was the pits because I was hotter than a two dollar pistol from the clothing wrapped tight on my body and slugging mud caked shoes through narrow rows didn't help my attitude.

Catching a glimpse of those people lugging heavy duty containers, with balsa wood and wire quart containers, made me want to run. I couldn't even lift my feet, let alone carry one of those ten ton baskets, but not to look like a pansy, I conceded. My options were to "sit in the car" or "shut up and get moving." It wouldn't have been so bad but I knew two cents a quart was a lot of work for not a lot of money. Trouble is I might have picked sixty quarts if I didn't eat every other strawberry. When asked what I was doing with the berries I said, "Nothing." My face told another story because my lips and mouth were bright red. Right then and there, my love for strawberries developed into a lasting companionship. My family and I went back numerous times to pick them.

My first taste of combining strawberries and crust was when I was around six years old. Mother was preparing the old fashioned, country style strawberry shortcake (not the kind with spongy cake) and I watched her every move. Chopping and mashing the red chunks made my mouth salivate, and the whiff of the plump red berries made me want to crawl inside the bowl. Each time she checked the pie crust, my eagerness grew intense. I had no idea what was about to transpire nor was I prepared for a taste of heaven. At last, the pie crust was golden brown, marbled with shortening, and a hint of salt hinged on the air as I fluffed the aroma into my face. The pie crust tempted me as I reached for a piece of the round morsel but then, as I watched mother layer the hot crust with a heaping cup of strawberries, my senses went into overdrive. The crust sizzled and steamed as the cold berries made contact and I was lost forever in the quest for strawberry shortcake. There was no hope for me because a taste of this precious, red jeweled crust had me in its clutches. I thought I had died, turbo charged by a strawberry, and gone straight to heaven.

This time of the year makes me lose sight of regular food. Somehow my eyes turn a shade of red, my nose tweaks in the direction of a berry and the oven is on full blast cranking out pie crust. My husband knows when the berry season comes around; there might as well be no other food in the house. Although he might frown at my insidious desire for strawberries, he has lovingly given me the "space" I need to devour the addictive, green capped, seed coated red sweet tasting morsels. Sometimes he surprises me with a crate of strawberries, secretly hoping I will get my fill. Since the season doesn't last too long, he appeases me and jumps for joy when the last berry is gone. Bless his heart. He never buys the frozen kind because he knows I won't eat them. It's either a fresh berry or no berry at all, something he learned a long time ago.

Newt Black and his strawberry patch are gone and so are those flesh seeking ticks and chiggers and long pants and long sleeve shirts. No mud caked shoes to scrape and no wood crates to tote. However, roadside vegetable and fruit stands pull me in like a magnet, and I can spot a strawberry sign a mile away. I won't hesitate for one minute to whip my car into a "buy strawberries here" parking lot to have a free for all, mad woman, strawberry frenzy.

When I was a child, I didn't choose to have this memory of strawberries... it chose me.

TO WEAR A POPPY

Memorial Day used to be called Decoration Day as it recognized those fallen soldiers before the end of the Civil War. Women of the south were seen placing decorations on many graves before it was pronounced a day of remembrance. No one actually knows the origin from where it gained popularity but many towns lay claim to its discovery. It's quite possible every town and citizen in the nation, whose loved ones died in a war within our country, declared their love to the fallen in some aspect. Wherever it began doesn't really matter because all soldiers, dying then and now, deserve respect and utmost admiration for the price they paid in valor.

On May 5, 1868, Memorial Day was officially proclaimed a national holiday when flowers were placed on the Confederate and Union graves in Arlington National Cemetery. It wasn't until New York City, in 1873, recognized it as a holiday to be remembered. Then in 1890, all the northern states followed suit. Unfortunately, the southern states refused to acknowledge the holiday and chose to honor their loved ones on a different day until after WWI, when all soldiers were honored, not just those dying in the Civil War. The battle, it seemed, was still raging even though it was over.

Many years ago, I read the poem "In Flanders Fields" written by John McCrae, a Canadian army physician. It was written for the WWI soldiers whose lives were lost while fighting the war on foreign soil. Flanders Fields battlefield is located in southern Belgium and north-west France but the cemetery in honor of the fallen soldiers and poem is in Waregem, Belgium. Three hundred sixty eight Americans are buried in this cemetery.

The poppy, by nature, will not bloom unless the seeds are disturbed. Even though they distribute seeds freely as their pods die, some of them can lay dormant for many years. When the war was raging on this battlefield, the poppy began sprouting. Foot traffic was so heavy the blossoms erupted with so much force; thousands of poppies awoke from their resting places. Blooms of red were everywhere in competition with the blood running deep from wounded and dying soldiers. Mr. McCrea was so moved with the beauty of the lovely flowers vying with death, he penned the poem. It is one of the most touching poems I have ever read and the tribute is lasting. The poem is in public domain in the United States and can be published.

"In Flanders fields the poppies blow
Between the crosses, row on row,
That mark our place: and in the sky
The larks still bravely singing fly
Scarce heard amid the guns below.

We are the dead: Short days ago,
We lived, felt dawn, saw sunset glow,

*Loved and were loved: and now we lie
In Flanders fields!*

*Take up our quarrel with the foe
To you, from failing hands, we throw
The torch: be yours to hold it high
If ye break faith with us who die,
We shall not sleep, though poppies grow
In Flanders fields"*

The paper poppy we see being sold by veterans was the brainchild of Moina Michael. John McCrae's poem inspired her to do more for the veterans. In penning her poem, <u>"The Miracle Flower,"</u> she chose the poppy because many sites of the war fields grew poppies and as the fields ran red with blood, so did the poppy. It is a symbol of recognition and one we should embrace. The poppy is so well known, it is used for various fund raising activities related to war orphaned children, disabled veterans and veterans funds.

In 1922, the VFW was the first veteran's organization to sell poppies on a national level and then two years later; the paper poppy was sold by the disabled veteran's through the "Buddy" Poppy Program. It is a worthwhile project for all the veterans and on every Memorial Day, I stop to purchase several of the meaningful tributes.

To the Veterans past, present and future, I salute you. You are heroes and I am proud to wear the poppy in recognition of your bravery.

If you wish to read about Moina Michael here is the link (source):

http://britishlegion-northstaffs.org.uk/history/moina_bell_michael.htm

Permission granted to use: In Flanders Field
http://www.gutenberg.org/wiki/Gutenberg:Permission_How-To

-- Greg Newby

Dr. Gregory B. Newby
Chief Executive and Director
Project Gutenberg Literary Archive Foundation
http://gutenberg.org
A 501(c)(3) not-for-profit organization with EIN 64-6221541
gbnewby@pglaf.org

COAL OIL LANTERNS

All of you who have read my stories know I love to look to the past, peer into the lives of those living without the amenities we use every day, and wonder how they managed to perform daily routines without stubbing their toe in the dark. I used to think I was born in the wrong century. Wrong! To wit, I bring you this question. Do you have a coal oil lantern? No, I am not referring to a bright, shiny, green or red Coleman lantern or the new fandangle battery operated lanterns. Those jig-whizzies are too easy unless the batteries are dead as a hammer and you are fumbling in the dark to find the right size to poke in the contraption. I am talking about the old fashioned, glass shade, hurricane lamps with a pull up wick and black belching smoke. The kind of smoke that will choke you to death before you can snap your fingers and uses coal oil, a.k.a., kerosene. The Hurricane's are "semi" old ... like me. It's brought to mind because of the latest power outage during the forceful winds shearing Bradford pear trees and shattering the nerves of people whose electricity went kaput.

We have several hurricane lamps as well as the other varieties of lanterns, and have used them when the electricity goes ka-thunk before night sets in and it's too early for bed. Playing cards by the light of a hurricane lamp was our pastime when the ice storm raged, leaving ice cubes dangling from naked trees and layers of ice crunching beneath the feet. Those all too few snowstorms we've had in the past allowed me to cook over the fireplace coals (I have an electric stove) and I loved the coziness it presented. Besides, there is comfort in seeing the first snow flake, all pristine and ready to blanket the ground with its loveliness. Wintertime leaves a body in anticipation because gusty winds might ... just might send snow. Hurricane lamps, snow and winter are companions.

Camping is fun as you sit by the glow and warmth of a campfire and tell ghost stories as children's eyes grow with the fear of someone yelling, "Boo!" A lantern flickers as though it has a tale to tell, and in a strange way, the reflections of a lantern are enchanting, almost hypnotic. Camping and lanterns go together, a thing you choose to do in the wild, not because the power has left you in a lurch. You don't worry about a refrigerator becoming rancid, the freezer warming up and melting ice cream, or how to maneuver in a dark house. Lucky for me I can see in the dark but my husband can't and his little toe connects with every door jamb in the house and he only shaves every other whisker. Believe me; you don't want to hear what he says.

Oh yes, I used to think how exciting it would be to live in a log cabin, cook on a wood stove, draw water from a well and go to bed when the chickens went to roost. However, (this is one giant however), this old, white haired bird has had a change of heart. Sure, I have cooked on a wood stove, drawn water from a well and been camping in sub-freezing and blistering hot temperatures. You might say I've been there, done that, and I ain't' a gonna do it a'gin'! If someone wants to remember the "good old days," turn off the air conditioner, open the windows and sweat out your brains!

I am used to having electricity, hot water, a stove to heat up in a moment's notice and all the niceties "pre" old age has to offer. It's those things we take for granted that we miss the most when we can't use it. My computer runs, the air conditioner flicks with a switch and the television blares if I want to see the news. You might say we are dead in the water without electricity and dependant on the over head wires casting shadows on the right of way. It seems, lately, all we have had is weather of unpredictable proportions.

I've had it with gale force winds, tornadoes, ice storms, thunderous rain rolling like the Arkansas River across my backyard, baseball size hail, sink holes the size of a small car in my front yard, pine cone missiles hurling at the speed of sound, tree limbs sticking in gutters, birds flying backwards and going nowhere, holes in roofs, upside umbrellas, people being hurt and killed by downed power lines, and whatever else is thrust upon unsuspecting nerve ends by Mother Nature plunging me into the black hole of the century. We've hauled off debris akin to Mt. Everest and it's not from cleaning weeds from flowerbeds or pruning trees. Enough already!

This summer, if the electricity plunges me in the dark, I am not going to sit on my laurels as I'm tired of trying to stay cool, tired of laying on tile floor to keep the sweat from rolling where it shouldn't or shifting positions to find a cool spot. I think I am going to pour out the coal oil, hide my hurricane lamps and go to a Motel 6 where they leave the lights on for you. At least I will have a TV to know when a storm is approaching, something cool to drink and air conditioned comfort. Here's to you, Tom Bodett!

Come winter I will say, "Hello hurricane lamps!"

YOUR FATHER ON FATHER'S DAY

Father's Day is an important way to let the man of the house realize how valued he is in his role as a parent. There are all kinds of fathers: a spiritual Father, single fathers, working fathers, idle fathers, grumpy fathers, and gentle fathers. Regardless of what their moniker is in the portrayal of life, they are like any other person wearing many hats. Although they might not show it in grandiose proportions with ooh's and ahs in a flower arrangement or say, "You shouldn't have," they have feelings and do enjoy rewards of being honored. Maybe it is gender oriented or a testosterone thing when they don't jump up and down when someone gives them a present, even a card, but they smile inward. It's a macho thing existing in most men not to show emotions.

My dad was one of the orneriest men alive, sometimes gruff and could scare the beejeebers out of anyone if he looked cross-eyed in a fit of temper. He was my dad and I loved him, regardless of the "temper or non-temper" of the day. Dad would come home from work, exhausted from tedious work at the smelter on Kibler Road and sit down and not move for several hours. He was grungy from head to toe and sometimes didn't look like the clean shaven dad I knew. Most men of my dad's era worked from sun up till sun down for meager wages but I never heard him complain. It was enough to sustain us as a family and kept food on the table and paid bills.

Then, when the smelting job ended, he began working for the Missouri Pacific Railroad as a Carman inspector. Some work hours included the swing shift and night work could be hazardous. Swinging a lantern and walking for hours up and down the railroad tracks, checking each and every box car for safety, made him tired. He would crawl under the trains every time one pulled into the yards. The yard was busy with trains coming in at all times during the day and night traveling from one state to another. It wasn't the job making him tired, as he loved being around the trains and sitting (when he could) near the roundhouse exchanging jokes with his fellow workers. He did not know if he would be "booted" for someone else with majority in the work force. In other words, being laid off because another man had been there the longest to take over dad's job was the problem. However, through thick and thin, grunge, black soot, mashed hands, broken ribs from lifting heavy equipment, bruises the size of baseballs and nearly having his eyes blinded, he continued to work. For many years, he did the same thing until he retired from Missouri Pacific.

Yes, I always told him Happy Father's Day and sometimes I would make him peanut butter cookies or a cake, decorated with his favorite, thick, chocolate frosting. It was just for him to let him know how much I loved him and to thank him for what he did for us as the bread winner. He didn't want the frou-frou stuff, or ties (he hated the throat croakers), and he didn't want flowers. He had plenty of tools, guns, ammo and fishing equipment. I suppose, for dad, a hug around the neck and a peck on the cheek would have been sufficient. He got those, too. Then, years after he retired, he became diabetic and the sweets stopped. All he wanted was a card and he got plenty of those. I think he kept everyone of them. Then, I wrote him letters about what he meant to me. He kept those, too. It didn't take much to make daddy happy. When I think of Father's Day, I think about him and all the good and bad times we had together.

Dad was a wealth of information and he told me when Father's Day became popular. He said it was possible it came about because of a Mother's Day celebration, inspired by Anna Jarvis. The first June Fathers Day was celebrated on June 19, 1910 in Spokane, Washington. In 1966, President Lyndon Johnson made June 19 a holiday for fathers but President Richard Nixon made it official in 1972. Who would have thought it would take so long?

My dad died on Sunday, August 15, 1996 and I miss his encyclopedia conversations. I miss his roaring belly laugh, risqué jokes, harmonica playing, feeding the ducks, his old blue truck, Big Smith overalls, faded mesh ball cap, his huge hands, prominent arched eyebrows, smelling the bluing for his gun cleaning apparatus, hearing him sing hymns, crazy antics, making sweets for him and hugging his neck and giving him kisses. I have those beautiful memories, and for now, it will sustain me.

This letter won't be read by my dad, but Happy Father's Day, J.D. Brannam. R.I.P.

A NORMAN ROCKWELL SKETCH

This time of year is for canning and it excites me to see all the jars of home canned goods lined up in my pantry. There is something special about hearing the lids pop indicating the jars have a proper seal. The only down side of canning is the crops are harvested at the same time, making for a haggard body. This year will be no exception but as long as I can provide good food for my family and friends, a little hard work is worth the effort. Besides, I really do enjoy canning.

On Tuesday, I went on a search and seizure for tomatoes as my vines are just now putting on the coveted red fruit. Yes, they are a fruit but we all call them vegetables. I don't care what they are called as long as I have them to satiate my hankering. As luck would have it, the Farmers Market in Fort Smith had none, and vendors of Van Buren said theirs would be ripe around July 1 or later. Trucking on down the road, I wound up on Highway 64 going east toward Alma. No roadside vendors ... rats! Deciding to go to my intended destination, I put aside my pity party, as tomatoes would have to wait and so would my yen.

I popped a cinnamon chew in my mouth and pretended it was a nice juicy tomato. It was red but the flavor left a lot to be desired. Exiting the parking lot of

Dr. Ronald Schlabach, my wonderful doctor in Alma, I thought of the renovated Farmer's Market open on Tuesday and Saturday. Wheeling my car toward the old, narrow, two lanes of Highway 64, I remembered traveling it when I was a child. Although I had not driven this route in many years, it still looked the same. There are endearing thoughts of wide-open farmland with cows roaming the lush grassy knolls.

Straw hats, plaid shirts and striped overalls captured my mind as I saw farmers waving to everyone. They knew no stranger. They sat on seats of old John Deere tractors plowing fields for preparation. Black smoke belched from the overhead exhaust pipes. An occasional woman, wearing a housedress and possibly a homemade sunbonnet atop her head, was hoeing a flowerbed. Dilapidated barns with vines entwining the rafters danced across the screen. The small bridge, near the curve of Alma's entryway, brought back visions of horrendous wrecks. I was looking in my rear view mirror of a time and place; long gone. All of these memories were picture perfect and colorful and reminded me of Norman Rockwell's sketches of human interest.

I had to stop for traffic before I could turn left into Alma. To my right was the old Farmers Cooperative and it was the place I used to go to find black Crowder pea seed ... not brown but genuine black Crowder. It is almost impossible to find them anywhere except for mail order. The traffic cleared as did my past treks to the Co-op. Not too far from the "T" (Alma's town entrance), I recognized the Farmer's Market. It is a large, pavilion structure with wood floors and ample space for numerous vendors. Today would be a good day for meeting several people. Three tables were set up with vegetables and houseplants neatly grouped for sale.

Behind one table was a group of youngsters. They had dark hair, big vivacious eyes and the beginning of a beautiful suntan. I noticed they were reading. Good for you, I thought ... smart kids. As I approached the table, they stopped what they were doing and asked if they could help me. The first thing I spied was a quart container of fresh English peas. My mouth began to water as I popped open a pod. The tender peas were as sweet as a chunk of candy and I bought them. I love the taste of raw English peas and it would be a miracle if I got home with any unopened pods. No tomatoes as expected, but yes, I hoped. Instead, I bought a passel of new red potatoes ... just the right size for canning. I asked the three girls if they liked to eat washed fresh-shucked corn, peas and okra ... uncooked ... straight from the garden. Surprisingly, they said yes. I told them it was the best way to eat them, sprinkled with a little celery salt. Dezirae Thomas, the pert child manhandling the scales, was delightful and talkative. Makinzee Thomas was in charge of the moneybox and the Rachel Thomas smiled a lot. A wee tot with the girls was trying in vain to shove a Dr. Seuss, Cat in the Hat book between the gaps in the wood floor. He did not succeed because of the eagle eye and loving supervision of Terry Thomas, the girls' grandmother. These children were learning valuable tools for life ... hard work, customer service, marketing, and distribution of money in how to correctly count back change to a customer. All of this they did with a smile. They were polite, happy children and as I drove out of the parking lot, I heard them yell, "Bye."

It was a lovely morning and now, because of these remarkable children and their grandmother, I have another picture perfect, Norman Rockwell sketch in my memory.

A FAVORITE FOURTH OF JULY

It was hot outside, so hot the metal on the bed of dad's truck would blister the skin right off the legs. Mother placed quilts in the bed and we sat down, eagerly waiting to move forward to our destination. Unfortunately, all of us kids were squeezed in like sardines between camping gear, pots and pans, and food to last for several days. We sat there, like little kids do, anticipating how far we would drive before we reached the camp site and eyeballed each other to figure how long it would take for one of us to throw the first punch. My sister, Hazel, my cousins and I sweated like pigs on a spit, but not to worry, we knew daddy would stop at Hay's Trading Post on 59 highway.

Pulling into the dirt parking area, daddy went inside to talk and pick up a few Fudgesickles. It would tide us over and cool us down till we reached the cool swimming hole near Devils Den Park. As the hot temperature hit the wrapper of the Fudgesickle, it adhered tighter than a cinched up corset. My Fudgesickle had a mind of its own and waited till my tongue and fudge merged. Fudge was dripping, so I gave it a good lick from the base upward. Heaven help me, my tongue stuck to the thing like glue and plastered the tip of my nose to the frozen delectable. I was hinged to a fudge bar and couldn't get loose. I couldn't talk and I couldn't breathe. All I could hear was laughter coming out of the nuts sitting next to me. My sister yelled, "Don't pull on it or you will rip the taste buds off your tongue." Another snickered, "Maybe it will keep her quiet." Lucky for me, the sun took pity and began melting the fudge faster than I could scarf it down. I was a mess. Chocolate was all over my face, down the front of my clothes and I was sticky. I think I must have invented the first Velcro face.

The wind blowing my long blonde hair into my face made matters worse. Each time I pushed the hair from my face, it felt like Scotch tape or wax jerking out unwanted whiskers. Not only that, but by the time we drove for an hour down the dirt road, I looked like a wide mouthed bull frog splattered by road kill.

The minute we pulled into the camping site, all of us kids leapt from the truck as though we were on fire. In a sense, we were! I was red as a beet but who would have known it? The chocolate prevented anyone from seeing my face ... except mother. The first thing out of her mouth was, "What on earth happened to you? You were clean when we left the house. I don't know how you can sit still and get dirty at the same time." I told her about the Fudgesickle attack.

Wouldn't you know it? We weren't able to go swimming. We had to help set up the camp and gather firewood and by the time it was finished it was getting dark. Dang it, I couldn't win for losing. Oh, well, we were there for the week-end and it would be fun come morning. Did I say morning? None of us got any sleep because I kept them awake. I kept hearing things go bump in the night and did a two step boogie with mosquitoes. I swear by all that is Holy, those blood suckers called their aunts, uncles, cousins, in-laws and outlaws to feast on me. When the sun came up I was nothing but a wad of knots, scratching and clawing as though I had been thrust in a nest of hornets. After the initial shock of trying to sleep on a cot and wondering what was going to jerk me up by the hair on my head, I smelled the most glorious, tempting aroma. It was breakfast.

The air was tempting. The morning dew tickled the sweet grasses and left a delightful breeze to cool the body. The firewood stoked the frying pan, sizzling lace on the most scrumptious eggs and bacon I ever tasted. It sent me into overdrive. I got my second wind and was raring to go. It was going to be the most fantastic Fourth of July ever imagined. Having my parents and sister, aunts and uncles, cousins and grandparents with me, firecrackers and sparklers to glow in the dark of night, a great swimming hole and fantastic cooks, what could be better?

Although Fourth of July is a national holiday to celebrate independence, I think of the Fudgesickles, dusty roads, swimming holes, my family ... and mosquitoes!

Have a safe, fun, and memorable Fourth of July, everyone.

THE ICE MAN

Go grab something cold to drink, put your feet up, and let's look back in time at a piece of long ago ... a refreshing necessity.

It was a beastly summer in 1955 but if you were like most kids, the heat wasn't an issue ... it was a way of life. It didn't matter if your face was drenched in sweat; dirt adhered to the creases of your eyelids, or those sweat-beads around the neck glistened with copper toned clay. We would play till we dropped, exhausted with red faces and sunburns, rest for a few minutes, and go, once again, full force under the old sol. During the day we'd play kick the can till our shoes had holes in them, King of the Mountain (I never was), Red Rover, roller skate on skates held together by string, or at night, swat at bats as they swooped toward objects we threw into the air.

We used our imagination or the toys we had to fulfill the lazy summertime vacation from school. The concrete sidewalk in front of my house, laid by my dad, ran the full length of our double lot, and offered a venue for playful kids. Our dirt road abutted the walk, but on the south end, a deep five foot slope from the downward pitch of the road afforded us a place to sit and dangle our legs. However, wearing shorts and sitting on the concrete usually created blisters on our backsides. It was hot, but we were happy as pigs in slop, and on occasion, I guarantee this personal note, we looked like pigs! It didn't matter to us because we didn't have a care in the world. We were happy-go-lucky kids.

We didn't have air-conditioning, or for that matter, knew what it was. We waited patiently on a cool wind or in desperation, go to the ice box, open the door and fan the icy, cold breeze. You heard me correctly, I said ice box. It wasn't a refrigerator but a large, white, heavy metal box with a double duty door and latch. At the bottom of the ice box was an area for large chunks of ice. Directly above the ice sat milk and eggs and other edibles. When the ice began to melt, all hands were on deck to mop up the impending water flow because the slide out tray beneath the ice box couldn't contain its contents. It was an aggravating mess.

Where did we get the ice chunks? On some days, all of us kids would gather at the foot of Henry Street and when we saw the old, dark blue truck lumbering up the boulder laden road, we would scream, "The ice man is coming. The ice man is coming!" Then, like all children, run as fast as we could to grab a piece of ice from the rear of the truck. I can remember the old tarpaulin draped across the ice to keep the dust from accumulating on the refreshing, soothing, cool treat. In order for the delivery man to know what pound of ice you needed, a small sign with the word "ICE" and various pound sizes was placed in a homeowner's front window. If an owner needed ice, the man would look at the sign, take out huge ice tongs, walk to the rear of the truck and grapple the size of ice needed. We watched, as the trickle of water slid from the massive cube, as he hauled it inside a house. Unbeknownst to the driver, while he was away from the truck, we would grab a few slivers of ice and pop them into our mouths. In short order the delivery was made, and the truck was nothing more than a speck on the horizon. We had our cold glass of ice water, and relished the rest of the day by swiping our foreheads with a chip of ice. I can still feel the delightful cool water dribble down my face.

After a phone call to the owner's son, he confirmed they owned the truck we enjoyed chasing. Capelle's Grocery and Ice Plant was situated at the corner of East Main and 13th Street, directly across from Jack's Motor Company. I remember riding in the back of my dad's truck as we drove to the ice plant. Even though I was told to stay in the truck, I didn't, and he usually found me sitting on the stoop, listening to the massive crunch as ice was being rammed into a giant auger. It was deafening, but oh, so cool. Just inside the building, ice was stacked in large heaps. Anyone wanting groceries or ice could go inside, pay the attendant and be on their way. I never saw anyone put ice in a container, but did see them fling it inside a car or rear of an old truck. If truth was known, the people buying the ice went in there to get cool as it was the only place in town where the air was crisp. I wanted to ask why they stood around taking in all the frigid temps (I was there because I liked the cool air) but they never did tell. I was nobody's dummy... it was hotter than H-E-double-hector outside and they liked the cold as much as I did. Capelle's Grocery and Ice House is no longer there but the memory lingers.

Now, I think I will go get a glass of ice from my automatic ice maker, fill it full of cold water from my refrigerator, sit back and enjoy the air-conditioned atmosphere of my house. No need to play King of the Mountain because I have a queen size chair and no one is going to shove me out of it.

LAKE LOU EMMA

Several months ago, Ronnie Ocker, a prominent business person, phoned me. His question was, "Do you know how Lake Lou Emma got its name?" I had to tell him no, although somewhere in the back of my mind, daddy had given me the information. For some reason, in the confines of my mind, the words "granddaughter" and "Bowlin" kept hovering over at me and I could hear daddy say, "You need to remember this!" It was one of those, in one ear and out the other, pieces of data he threw out for me to remember. I knew the lake had been there for umpteen years (long before my time) and I did remember the completion date of the dam. It was 1956. I remember going with daddy to watch the large dozers reconstruct the land. Not hard to understand its purpose because the raging waters, flowing from the lake during a rain storm deluged Rena Road making it almost impassable. Rena Road, like many in the town, was dirt and quite narrow. Many times a car would be swept off the road during a heavy rain. It was a precarious area and dangerous. I don't remember anyone dying but they came close.

Curious, I did a quick search on the web but turned up nothing. Nowhere does it state the name to which it got its moniker but general information such as latitude, longitude, degrees minutes / seconds and tons of maps. It is owned by the Crawford County Conservation League and is used for recreation purposes such as arts and crafts fair and the children's fishing tournament. Lake Lou Emma is Crawford County property and not a part of the incorporated city of Van Buren. Lake Lou Emma Dam is of earthen construction. Its height is 20 feet with a length of 550 feet. Its capacity is 120 acre feet. Normal storage is 80 acre feet. Nice to know but not why it was named Lake Lou Emma. A trek to the lake didn't turn up any plaque to squash my curiosity. Why is one not there?

I emailed a person at the Crawford County Conservation District. She didn't know the answer and put me in contact with someone who might know the answer. When I phoned him, he was sure he had the information and would get back with me. Well, he never contacted me! Going to the library didn't turn up any information but I did find other articles tweaking my memory. I searched for a telephone listing for the Crawford County Historical Society. I came up empty handed. The Crawford County Court House is going through upstairs renovation and the answer wasn't there. I asked people at the Van Buren Municipal Complex and they didn't know. They did give me two numbers to phone. One number I didn't phone (did that once and wasn't going to do it again), but did phone another one. He told me he thought the last name was Bowlin or Bowling but wasn't for certain.

A Picture Frame of Memories, Book I

I was getting somewhere. The word Bowlin wasn't a dream. Then a phone call went to someone else but he couldn't be positive. Two people confirmed the last name for the original owner of the lake was Cosma Bowlin. Halleluiah! Now, my intensity for finding out the person for which the lake was named has turned into an all out compulsion.

Disgusted and becoming more impatient, I phoned a man whom I learned was with the Crawford County Historical Society. He and his sweet mother have gone through mega amounts of data to no avail. Hearing the lake might have been named for a granddaughter of a person in the county, I phoned them. She said, "No, it would be nice but it's not true." She gave another name to contact. No such luck there! Quite by accident, I rang a person I knew from my church. We had a pleasant conversation and she told me another person to contact. Alas, no answer there. Blast it all, my sister couldn't even remember. Aarrrrk, I am having a meltdown and at my age too many meltdowns are going to do me in.

You would think someone in this small town would have the answer. It appears it is part of a conspiracy; part of the X-Files squirreled inside the catacomb dungeon of a musty, old, military basement, sixty feet under the ground, surrounded by heavy duty bars and armed guards. Is it national security information? Was there a fight over this property? Did someone commit mayhem to secure this property? Why, if it is county property, is there businesses situated there. Who owns those franchises? Do they pay county, city or both taxes? What, for crying out loud, what?

So help me Hanna, one way or another I will find out the mystery of Lake Lou Emma. The answer to this elusive question is out there somewhere and I will uncover it.

To be continued....

Source:
http://findlakes.com/lake_lou_emma_arkansas~ar00490.htm

PART TWO OF LAKE LOU EMMA

Saturday morning, after my story on Lake Lou Emma appeared, pennies–bright, shiny, copper pennies began pouring into my hands. Pennies from heaven are generally thought of as those messages from the beyond, from loved ones sending cryptic messages to those left behind to assure them they are all right. The messages, from eighty-three years young to present day, were from earthly pennies–direct descendents of Cosmo Bowlin and friends who remembered the answer to my question. Some were fond remembrances of time spent at Lake Lou Emma. I thank all of you for taking the time to read my article as it seems to have touched the hearts of many.

The phone rang while I was reading the Press-Argus Courier. Jolting a part of my memory, she told a story about a lovely family. I told her I knew all of them through St. John's United Methodist Church. When the mother of two children passed away, this wonderful lady relating the story to me, was there for the boys, helping them maintain composure and giving them the love and attention they needed. It was a traumatic time for two small boys whose beloved mother was no longer with them. Happy conversations centered on Lake Lou Emma and how the boys, their mother and grandmother were a part of its heritage. Are they? In another story, after I confirm the truth, I will let you know. So far with this fine piece of thread, these four pennies of possible heritage, are stitching one corner of a patchwork quilt.

Several other persons (eight) phoned me telling me to contact various citizens of Van Buren. A couple from Uniontown phoned and related fine words to me about the lake. Her husband's father, who is deceased, would be over 100 years old and passed down to his relatives, all the answers to my questions. They echoed the same answers I had received earlier. Before I hung up the phone, I knew they were wonderful people and I told her to hug her husband's neck for wanting to share his knowledge with me. Now, the quilt has another corner and the pennies keep amassing.

The golden thread to stitch another corner came from an eloquent man. He told me Tales of the Crypt, held in Fairview Cemetery 2007, featured the life of William Bowlin as portrayed by a fine actor. He said it was fascinating to learn about the Bowlin family and how generations of Bowlins' contributed to the city of Van Buren.

The sides of the quilt were coming together by another thread. I remembered this caller and how beautiful she was as part of the royal home coming court of Van Buren High School's football team. Her sister and I went to school together. She told about her father telling the family to get in the car and they drove to Lake Lou Emma. It was winter and the lake would be frozen for ice skating. Stepping on to the ice, he plunged through and their ice skating event was over. We laughed and she continued telling me recollections about the history of the lake.

One of the pennies to phone was the center of the quilt, the core of existence and knew the reason behind Lake Lou Emma and its namesake. By now, probably all readers of the Press- Argus Courier know or think they know the answer but it won't be divulged in this particular story. Some of you will be surprised to learn the name and why it was named Lake Lou Emma. I assure you, I do have the answer but its heritage and everything relating to Lake Lou Emma will be told in another feature. As I understand, the story is vast and I don't want anything to be misconstrued or taken out of context. There is a comprehensive book, complied by a direct descendant, detailing the lives and heirs of the Bowlin family. Before my story will be printed, the gentleman who phoned me will have first eyes on the story to approve, edit or discard.

Right now, I won't reveal the last golden thread or the name of the remarkable penny. Until the quilt can be stitched to perfection, it will be a secret. Stay tuned, as this glorious patchwork quilt will unfold ... right before your eyes and the bright copper pennies will glow.

Joyce L. Rapier

LAKE LOU EMMA SAGA

In Tennessee, 1835, when Noble Bowlin (patriarch) died, his widow (matriarch) Catherine (Cliff) Bowlin wed John Barnes. After his death in 1843, (also in Tennessee), Catherine Barnes, her seven children and brother-in-law, Robert McCurry, boarded a flat bottomed boat. It was autumn when the leaves were falling at a rapid rate and temperatures plunged to an unbearable degree. Not knowing what they would encounter must have been a harrowing experience. They floated down the Mississippi River to the mouth of the Arkansas River where they climbed aboard a steamboat and landed in Van Buren on March 10, 1844. Van Buren, Arkansas was their residence until her death in 1868 at age sixty-two.

One of her children was William Bowlin, around twelve or so, when they made their way to Van Buren. When he turned eighteen, he worked as an apprentice in a printing office. From there, he continued with Arkansas Intelligence, another publishing business established by Absalom Clark. Some of his businesses included a liquor store and dry goods. At this point in his life, he entered the Federal Army.

Imagine a misty morning, the eyes trying to focus on surrounding danger and men fighting in the Civil War ... the blue and the gray. Heavy with gunfire, not knowing if your relative is among the casualties or if you are face to face with kin fighting for the other side. It happened more often than not, as the American Civil War was pitted and scarred with more than territorial boundaries. At stake were the opinions, right or wrong, of those who couldn't see eye to eye on political reform. It would take more than opinions but death–death of 600,000 soldiers to change the arena of these fighting men. The American Civil War is known to be the greatest war in history with more than three million men harboring hatred for one another. This was the United States but nowhere was it united.

There were infantrymen, whose bloody feet trod over boulder laden mountains, securing the way through heavy forested areas and hoping beyond hope they would return to their families. Most of them didn't. Cavalrymen were in limited supply during the onset of the war but gradually increased for both sides. Their duties included guarding railroads and supply trains and escorts for generals. A cavalryman's' first priority was the care of his horse as without his steed, he became a foot soldier. Those duties, with or without his mount, didn't keep them from becoming a casualty.

Van Buren resident and former Knox County, Tennessean, and Union (north) Captain William Bowlin was one of those cavalry survivors. After helping drive Confederate General Price from Missouri in 1864, Bowlin received his discharge from Memphis, Tennessee. Later, he returned to Van Buren to resume the business he established and try his hand at farming. Amassing over 1,000 acres, a vast portion of land was used in farming. Being a stockholder and director of Citizen's Bank, he was proud, accomplished, and entrepreneurial for his time and an astute businessman. It is my understanding, the Bowlin home place was where the Press-Argus Courier is now located.

In the year 1852, he married a beautiful woman from Missouri. Her name was Samantha (Samanthy) Neal. Their children's names were Rebecca (John Clark), Noble, James, Lillie (LaFayette Wright), Joseph, Fannie (John O'Brien), and Elizabeth (James Lowery). Twenty-eight year old Samanthy died in 1860. To avoid more confusion of heirs, I will cut to the chase and fast forward.

Noble Bowlin, a child from William Bowlin's first union, was married to Lou Emma Mills. Troy, their son, was married to Hattie Humphrey. They were the parents of Julia (Bowlin) Woolley, one of the "possible heirs" and "tongue-in-cheek - happy conversations" remark, I had with Nancy Dunham Helmer, and wrote about about in part two. It is fact. To my knowledge, Julia had a son and daughter. The daughter, Judy Kupers, passed away leaving two small boys, Jeff and David Kupers.

Noble and Lou Emma also had a son named Cosma. Cosma was married to Lucille Jordan and their son's name was Cosmo (a) P. Bowlin. His wife's name was Lois. Are you as confused as I am with all these names, dates and heirs? Good! Now I am going to reveal the answer to the question so we all can move forward.

A Picture Frame of Memories, Book I

In 1955, eighteen acres, in and around the perimeter of a lake, were sold by Cosmo and Lois Bowlin to the Crawford County Conservation League, Inc. for the sum of $2,500.00. According to the deed, on record in the Crawford County Courthouse: "This deed is made subject to the agreement and understanding that said lake shall continue to be named & called Lake Lou Emma & it is further agreed between the parties hereto that in the event said property ceases to be used for a public purpose or if the name of the same shall be changed or if said property ceases to be open to the public for their use the same shall immediately revert to the grantors herein, their heirs assigns & administrator. It is understood between the parties that the grantees shall have the right to use the proceeds from concessions or business which is proper, beneficial and suitable to a part area for improvement of the premises or for a similar use either on the property or elsewhere." The lake was named for Lou Emma Mills, wife of Noble, mother of Cosma, grandmother to Cosmo and daughter-in-law to William.

All these pennies are shining brightly and the quilt has been completed because of those persons contacting me. A special thanks to John Chitwood who provided the history of his ancestors. Please clip this column and save it for some other unsuspecting soul who asks you the question. "Do you know how Lake Lou Emma got its name?" Whew! I'm back to the regular scheduled stories. I've got a headache and need some coffee.

WPA

It began with President Herbert Hoover and the U.S. Congress in 1932 as Reconstruction Finance Corporation because of The Great Depression of the United States. People were hard pressed to find any kind of job as the stock market crashed and banks closed. It was a time of desperation for families as they saw their livelihood come crashing to the ground. This program gave a glimmer of hope to millions of people as jobs were activated in various projects. Reconstruction Finance Corporation led the way to road constructions, literacy programs, erecting public buildings, and distribution of food, housing and clothing to those desperate for help. It was the beginning of the WPA.

Works Progress Administration, (WPA), was initiated in 1935 by President Franklin Delano Roosevelt by presidential order, and would continue to help literally millions of people in a relief program. Although it was set up in April 1935, it wasn't activated until July of that year by congressional funding. By 1938, WPA employed 3.3 million people. Rules were thirty hours per week but most of the jobs lasted months on a site which allowed them to eat and sleep on the site. Hourly wages were based on the area, the person's skill and urbanization. A typical pay was from $19.00 to $94.00 per month. Its total estimated expenditure by the year 1941 was a whopping $11.4 billion. Of that money, over $4 million dollars were spent on inner city streets, highways, and rural roads and more than $3 billion combined on each of the public owned utilities and public buildings and welfare.

By 1940, the WPA was winding down, and like any government procedure, changed courses. Factories were increasing and specific vocation training came into play. Unemployment dropped as men and women prepared their change in lifestyle. Up till World War II, WPA had the largest employment base in our country. WPA was officially closed in 1943.

There were, as usual, those who believed the WPA was a ridiculous situation in that expenditures wasted tax dollars on frivolous projects. Some even went so far to say that President Roosevelt was making his own "political machine" through the back breaking jobs men and women toiled. In Harper Lee's 1960 classic novel, ***To Kill a Mockingbird***, it even mentioned Maycomb County's proverbial idle resident as "the only person fired from the WPA for laziness."

Typical, judgmental slurs during the WPA are no different from what we hear today with programs helping those less fortunate. Back then, I could fathom persons having the "gold brick" syndrome, milking it for all its worth, just as people have the wherewithal to know how to skirt and maneuver rules on today's programs. It's a fact of life and people are people.

I wasn't born during the WPA but those persons having lived through it would be about seventy-six plus in years. My daddy is included in those persons and he did work for the WPA. Daddy told us times were hard and food was scarce for those without money, so people took work wherever they could find it and weren't too proud to dig ditches. When we asked about what he did for the WPA he showed us. He took me and my sister to see some of the bridges he helped build in Mountainburg. If they haven't been razed or improved, they are situated on the road going to the old Lake Fort Smith and in and around the area. Made of concrete, many of them have WPA stamped on the end of the pillars. If you will notice the small, concrete barriers on each side of a road where many ditches run through the road and parallel to it, those were built by the WPA. A picture I have shows daddy driving a bulldozer to help clear rough terrain to build the electric right of way in rural areas. In our area, if you see a very old clearing where electric lines flow down a mountainside, many of our local citizens helped build it. If it weren't for the WPA and men and women's backbreaking work, some of these projects wouldn't have been completed.

For all of you, whose relatives are still living, ask them about what they did during The Great Depression. They are here for a reason, have a wealth of information tucked away in their memories, and because of their tenacity, we all could learn a valuable lesson in how they survived. Write everything down while you still have a chance as history has a way of repeating itself. Their story is a story to be told, and who knows, they might have the key to unlock future doors to keep us from repeating another Great Depression.

Source:
http://en.wikipedia.org/wiki/Works_Progress_Administration

Joyce L. Rapier

GOING TO THE MOVIES

It might have been hot as a jalapeño pepper outside or cold as a well digger in January, but come Saturday our feet did the walking. We were oblivious to anything but our destination, our tunnel vision entertainment. It was the Bob Burns Theatre. It was noisy and squirming with kids of all ages. It didn't matter what was showing, but the fact was, two full length movies kept us occupied for a complete afternoon. We didn't have to worry about X rating or if the movie had any offensive language. We didn't see anyone prancing on the wide screen, naked as a Jay bird, or bed scenes that would make you gasp or strings of expletives flowing off the tongue. It was unheard of at the time. The only thing "sticky" was tromping through spilled soft drinks, paper cups and listening to the scrunch of popcorn beneath our feet. The silver screen was as clean as a whistle, but not so for the aisles of the Bob Burns Theatre. Trash receptacles? Yes, trash receptacles were in the theatre, but they didn't hold too many candy or hot dog wrappers, popcorn containers or soft drink cups.

A general admission price for the theatre was fifteen cents with enough money left over for a hot dog and a box of popcorn. If a kid had twenty-five cents, they were up-town. Feature that in comparison to today's prices, not to mention the cost of popcorn and a soft drink. Saturday's were double feature day and the kids were lined up in droves to get inside the theatre. Centered at the entrance was the ticket booth where a young female sat. She would take our money and we rushed through the "in" doors. To the right of the entrance was the concession stand full of hard to select candies and mouth watering treats. The balcony (entrance on the east side) was "reserved" (what a travesty) and the restrooms were upstairs on the west side of the building.

My favorite area for sitting was down the left side of the aisle, mid way between the poles supporting the balcony. Sometimes a scuffle would ensue between those wanting to sit four feet from the screen. I am sure they went home with a neck ache and blurry eyes. Our feature for the day might have been a couple of Roy Rogers / Dale Evans westerns with several cartoons thrown in for good measure. It might have been, *Francis the Talking Mule.*

Bud Abbott and Lou Costello's, *Go to Mars* or the movie where they *Meet the Mummy,* left you rolling in the aisles. Many of the Bud Abbott and Lou Costello movies were full length, running nearly two hours. The comedy duos', *Who's on First,* is the most popular and remembered routine of their career. *Who's' on First* was inducted into the Baseball Hall of Fame, but sadly, the men, who made the tongue twisting comedy, were not.

Godzilla, a four hundred foot monster shattered the decorum of the theater. Eyes grew large and popcorn could be seen flying through the air when an underwater atomic bomb, being tested off the coast of Japan, awakens the slumbering, prehistoric monster out of hibernation and through its fit of anger, attacks Tokyo. Talk about screams! Everyone in the theater went berserk. Most of the females screamed bloody murder and headed for the concession stand. Some of the boys scooted lower in their seats and only raised their heads to make sure the monster wasn't going to leap out and grab them. *Godzilla* was supposed to be giving *King Kong* a run for its money and would replace the giant ape as the movie of all times. Watching *King Kong* scale the Empire State Building while Faye Wray flailed in the ape's hand was almost sad. The great ape knew her life was at stake and placed her on the ground before he was surrounded by airplanes and killed. The graphics and sound effects of the times were phenomenal but can't hold a candle to the present day surround-sound and technological, graphic, computer enhanced, visual effects making you jump out of your skin.

Sci-Fi movies and *Tom Corbett's Space Cadet* and crew of the Polaris ventures filled the theatre. It was the precursor of today's *Star Trek. Frankenstein,* considered to be one of the best science fiction movies, was written by British novelist Mary Shelly in 1818. Robert Louis Stevenson's 1886 novel, *Dr. Jekyll and Mr. Hyde*, vampire and zombie "b" movies, Bram Stoker's, *Dracula,* and other amazing ventures filled our Saturday afternoon. After seeing one of these horror shows, you hoped it would still be daylight outside. If not, it was a race to see who could get home faster. Without some great novelists, these and other movies would never have been viewed.

We still have the theatre but with another moniker, The King Opera House. It's been revamped with no silver screen or concession stand. The restrooms are on the first floor for convenience. Now great plays are for viewing, and who knows ... in several years some of these stage performers could be the next generation Sci-Fi producers. Go for it and entertain us.

COMIC BOOKS

Comic books weren't just for children. They were read by millions of men and women, too. It was a past time filled with excitement and fun and only cost a nickel to fifteen cents per book, depending on the most popular at the time. Albeit, some were a bit risqué (reserved for adults) but for the most part, children could escape through adventures as wild as the mind could conceive. None were dangerous sorts but engaged the mind to a fantasy land of make believe worlds. In my opinion, comic books were not evil, filled with sorcery, nor did they put children in harm's way. They did not create havoc for destruction or produce wild, demonic children out of control.

Comic books were simply pieces of the time, a get away from the mundane side of life and repose. By design, most of them were serial and delighted folks to find the latest release. It was not uncommon to see people searching through stacks of comic books to find one they hadn't read. They were exchanged by neighbors but always returned if they were "borrowed." People respected other people's property and returned how they were received. Clips of dialogue, side by side on each page, didn't make people think they were sitting down to a long and grueling overture of tiny print. Most were in color, with large print, humorous and only several pages to peruse. Comic books made people read. It was considered a national pastime.

One of my all time favorites was Chester Gould's, *Dick Tracy*. It delved into the 1930's, Chicago, crime fighting character everyone enjoyed. Dick Tracy was the ultimate crime fighter, always with the theme that everything is "good or bad." There were no gray lines entering the picture. In Dick Tracy's world, you were either good or bad and paid the price if you crossed the line. You never had to figure out who did the crime as there were no "whodunits" in his vein of search and seizure.

Some of the *Dick Tracy* comics were considered a tad noir. It had a dark side of humor, a quirk and designing brilliant touch of the creator's vivid imagination. Gould's character villains took the limelight in monikers such as, Shoulders, a narcissistic male who wouldn't believe no women hated him. He thought he was the ultimate gift to women. Flattop Jones was a hit man and blackmailer for underworld crime. Flattop's name gave visualization when he popped into a clip as the top of his head was flatter than a pancake and his eyebrows were one continuous black streak. Before Flattop and Dick Tracy collided in an unprecedented hail of gunfire, he was the public's number one loved and hated villain. Pruneface was a Nazi spy, machine engineer and nerve gas aficionado.

He also gave Dick Tracy a run for his money but in the end, met his maker. One of the most ingenious inventions hailed from the comic book character was the two-way wrist radio and its comic book inventor, Diet Smith. Some people could say the "make believe" two-way radio, invented in this strip, was the pioneer of real life police equipment. Tess Trueheart was Dick Tracy's girlfriend of eighteen years, who he finally married. Their children, Junior and Bonnie Braids went on to find wild journeys through the excitable comic strip. When the comic strip became space oriented and off the wall, it gradually went by the wayside.

On a lighter note and away from the crime scenes were the comedies of *Archie* and his cohorts, Jughead, Veronica and Betty. *Little Lulu* and Tubby and Iggy were rotund, philosophical, speak-your-mind characters. Some of the quips used in *Little Lulu* might have been perceived as barbs. *Blondie, Little Orphan Annie* and others in this category delved on the human aspect of life and touched on relationships. The ethereal, *Casper the Friendly Ghost,* captured the hearts of many readers. Casper's quest to conquer and allay the scary side of ghosts, befriended a small child with his whimsical antics. He always let the good shine through his deeds. The powerhouse type of comics included *Superman, Batman, Wonder Woman, Captain Marvel* and other phenomenal, super strength heroes. Westerns had *Davy Crockett, Sisco Kid, Roy Rogers, Gene Autry,* and the *Lone Ranger*. There was a vast array of comic books to be read. Some people hoarded a series of their favorites, and now, many years later are considered collector items. How many of you still have a copy or two of your favorites?

If we search deep enough, somewhere ... in the archives of our minds, we will find a long lost, comic book friend.

OLD WIVES TALES

Has your nose itched lately - maybe the right side or the left? Did you expect to have a visitor and it didn't happen? Those two go together as a tale of lore. I wonder how many times we heard those words and why it began. Supposedly if the right nostril itched, you could expect a female visitor or if the left side it would be a male. What happened if the whole nose went on a rampage and itched for an hour? Would you have a whole clan of relatives knock at the door?

What about umbrellas? If you opened it inside a house seven years of bad luck would follow you everywhere you trod because someone you loved was going to die. I remember having a plastic umbrella when I was small and deliberately opened and closed it inside the house. Mother came unhinged telling me someone would die and the curse of bad luck would be held over my head. It was a bunch of hooey! The only bad experience I have had with umbrellas is having it turn inside out in a torrential downpour or having water shoot through my shoes when I closed it trying to get inside a car. An occasional jab with the sharp pointed top is about the only misfortune I ever encountered.

Did you ever walk on a sidewalk but never stepped on the cracks? How about the oval imprints etched in the walkway in downtown Van Buren? The etchings were at a corner of every other section of the sidewalk indicating the person or company who laid the concrete. Did you ever stomp on them yelling, "One, two, three, good luck for me?" Those expansions in the sidewalk were taboo. Kids screamed, "Step on a crack, you'll break your mother's back." Half of the time, the sidewalks were so full of natural cracks; we walked on the dirt roads dodging potholes and rocks.

Have you ever played horseshoes? You know the game where a stake is driven into the ground and you toss those clunkers to see who could get a ringer. It's a wonder a horse can lift those metal taps because they are heavier than a pound of lead. Anyway, a horseshoe is supposed to have good luck if it is nailed to the top of a door. Mind you, it has to be nailed in the center of the door with the round portion at the bottom. Good luck settles into the shoe and keeps evil spirits from floating out of it. What happens if the nail rusts and it falls? All you will have is an evil, heavy duty horseshoe cracking your skull. Believe it or not, a horseshoe hangs at the top of my backdoor. Not because of luck, evil sprites or spirits but because it's an old relic and I don't have a horse.

If you break a mirror, look out because your luck is going to go down the tubes. Another seven years of bad luck? Not to worry because if you bury it in the backyard on a moonlit night all of your good luck will be returned. The only bad luck a person might have is cleaning up the mess and not being able to see if your hair is combed properly.

Don't cross your eyes because they will get stuck, or stop cracking your knuckles, it'll make your fingers wider than your hand. If you swallow a wad of gum it will stick to your ribs and you won't digest it for seven years. If your right hand itches, don't scratch it as money is about to be given to you but if your left hand itches you'd better scratch it or money is going out of your pocket. If your left ear rings, someone is talking about you in a good way. If the right ear rings, bad things are being said. This is where "Good talk on, bad stop" originated. By the way, I am not referring to tinnitus ... a medical condition of constant ringing or buzzing in the ears.

Do you practice pulling turkey wishbones on Thanksgiving and Christmas? It's a fun tradition to pull on the wishbone with another person to see who can get the longer half. This tradition and lore has been around for years as it is said if you make a wish, the wish will come true. I wonder what the turkey wished.

I collect wind chimes and bells. There is an old wives tale about those, too. It appears bells are to ward off evil and the gentle sound of wind chimes keep demons at bay. Personally, my idea is not of evil but of good thoughts. Whenever a bell rings, someone in heaven gets their wings and wind chimes are those angels singing with golden harp accompaniment. This is a better way to think of a delicate, melodious china or metal bell or hearing wind chimes broadcast glee on a breezy day.

Folklore has been around for centuries. Some of the old sayings may have a ring of truth to them such as, an apple a day keeps the doctor away. Other pieces of lore are exactly that ... lore. It's a fun thing to remember and keep alive those wacky things we heard as a child. The list of sayings are priceless and a way of keeping a touch of hilarity in our lives.

Now, I will cross my fingers and make a wish. It's that all of you think of as many old wives tales as you can to bring happy memories to your hearts.

Joyce L. Rapier

OLD GROCERY STORES

Searching through microfiche at the Van Buren Public Library, I came across an interesting fact. It wasn't what I was looking for but it piqued my interest enough to make me search further. The years 1932 - 1935 on this microfiche came alive.

The Press-Argus, May 4, 1934, was brimming with interesting stories, some captivating me and others not so much. Not because the stories didn't have meaning for the day but that I didn't know the persons in question. What caught my attention were various ads and tidbits a person might find in the current day, Press-Argus Courier.

This beautiful ad was compliments of A.W. Tate and Sons. The grocery store was in the exact place where Tate's Flower and Gift Shop stands today. The small grocery ad was part of the newspaper, not a flyer. These items and prices are what I read. How would you like to buy a dozen, country fresh eggs for fifteen cents or cured ham hock for ten cents a pound? Cheddar cheese was eighteen cents per pound and a pound of oleo was twelve cents. It didn't stop there. Fresh asparagus was ten cents a bunch and a large head of lettuce was only ten cents. A couple of staples were low-priced. A large bottle of catsup only cost fifteen cents and a box of crackers was twenty-two cents. A large can of green beans was ten cents. Compare these to the prices we pay today. It seems like very little money for those goods but prices are relevant to the times. This was 1934 and the Great Depression was still making people despair. While some could afford, others could not.

On this reel, I counted a listing for numerous grocery stores. They were T. Guy Reed and Son, T. J. Garner, Arkansas Grocery, Grover C. Neal, Everett's Meat Market, and S. J. Harshbarger. I have no clue where the majority of them were located as the address was not given. Harshbarger's Grocery Store was on the north corner of twelfth and East Main Streets. It was right across the street (toward the west) from A.W. Tate and Sons where the parking lot of the First Baptist Church stands. These and other grocery stores in Van Buren were probably feeling the pinch as the Great Depression raged and it would be interesting to know how many grocery stores went out of business as people couldn't afford to shop their establishment.

To stave off depression for those persons perusing the paper, The Press-Argus must have been keenly aware as to what would ease the reader. Articles for women were in each issue, sports venues for the masculine, crosswords (one of my daily rituals), and several comic strips to help alleviate stress. Some of the comic strips were The Flatheads, S'Matter Pop, Keeping up with the Joneses, and Finney of the Force. It was hard to read the captions of the microfiche comic strips and doubly hard to read some of the articles as newspaper fades with age. As usual the newspaper was filled with obituaries, people running for political offices, and small communities (Figure

Five, Turner, etc.) and world news. It was brilliant to preserve a piece of the past. Kudos.

Comparing the long ago grocery store ads to those of today is daunting but surprisingly similar. The items listed would be those you might see in a current flyer, albeit price change. Then, as I think about it, in seventy-four years, the prices are relative. We aren't in a Great Depression but the price of gasoline and cost of goods to produce and transport places a lot of us in the same category as those living in 1934. Depending on the brand a person buys today, I might say we are running parallel with the former years. Yesteryears price of green beans at ten cents a can and today's generic brand costing approximately sixty-nine cents is still a bane on the pocketbook but the comparison in can sizes strains it even further. It is approximately 3% inflation since 1934 for those making sixty-five cents per hour to those making minimum wage today. However, many people were earning only one dollar per day in 1934 and its percentage would be astronomical.

In the 1950's, Van Buren's Main Street was alive with mom & pop grocery stores. All of them were scattered up and down the street and a few on side streets. A person didn't have to walk very far to purchase groceries and you knew the proprietor's first name. In 2008, things have changed dramatically as there are no grocery stores on the main drag. Some establishments, out of Van Buren proper, have a few shelves containing groceries and it is convenient to pop in and out if you are in a hurry, but count them ... only three are actual grocery stores and one is a super center.

The past seventy-four years is history and things have changed. Seventy-four years from now citizens might pay five dollars just to look at the label ... who knows, they may be eating labels! I won't be looking at microfiche or writing this column. The horror of it all but it's relative.

TEEN TOWN

As I walked through the aisles of a store, Bobby Vinton was crooning, *Blue Velvet.* It was caressing the shoppers. It was alluring me to sink into the suave, melodious, Bebop and swing time of Teen Town. It was November 29, 1956, (microfiche The Press-Argus), when we learned KFSA was going to build a television tower on Mount Vista and their plans to construct a road to it. It was situated on the apex of the mountain and dead ended at its west area. It was a first for our vicinity and would increase areas for new houses and redirect access roads.

At the time, Mount Vista was a dirt road, twisting and turning like a centipede through a piece of untouched forest. It was precarious in some spots because the road veered dangerously close to the cliffs. Curious to see the building, many people ventured up the mountain, dodging deep ditches so they wouldn't careen down the treacherous embankment. More often than not, cars would meet on the curves scattering rocks and dust in all directions as brakes were engaged.

When teenagers found out the small building would hold a Teen Town, word spread like wildfire. Teen Town was exactly how it sounded, a dance arena for Van Buren and Fort Smith teens. It was controversial in that some people thought dancing would entice children / teenagers to revolt against their parents and sway them away from church. Some rumors told it was "ungodly" to twist and turn in front of a camera. Cheek to cheek dances would surely send us all to hell. This myth, of our youth being damaged, was nothing more than fear monger. We did not revolt against our parents and continued to go to church. All of us teenagers thought there was nothing wrong in enjoying a part of our youth, especially when most of our parents danced to the big band era. It was a craze, just like the 40's, but we had to prove we were not rebellious and at the same time rebel against rumors. Like most 1950 teens, the majority was good but as usual some would push the envelope to see if they could destroy fun for the rest of us. Teenagers were in a catch twenty-two.

It was a time of the Bop, Hand Jive *(Oh, can you hand jive?),* the Stroll, slow dances and Swing held over from the 40's. Sock hops made you move furniture; rugs and anything else on a floor, just to put the needle down and spin those records. Some dances were in groups and others with a partner and what better way to enjoy the dances when you heard ... "Teen Town, it's coming to you live from KFSA."

All the girls would doll up with crinolines (can-cans - layers upon layers of mesh petticoats), Poodle Skirts (usually made out of felt), and white Bobby socks with penny loafers or oxfords. Sweaters were the norm back then or maybe a white blouse. Most all girls wore belts around their waists, some narrow, others wide. Ponytails, done up with rubber bands, flipped through the air. Spit curls, with a Bobbi pen holding them in place till they dried, swirled in all directions ...

much like the sideburns on a young boy. Sometimes midi skirts would be worn. In order to walk properly without falling over your own feet, a slit up the back afforded some comfort.

The boys wore rolled up Levis. It had to be Levis to look cool. One or two rolls from the ankle exposed white socks with wing tip loafers and taps. The taps were nailed to the heel of the shoe and clicked and clacked when feet hit anything solid. Some boys wore suede shoes and if they were preppy, a narrow tie or clip on. A white shirt or white tee to show off the masculinity bedecked all of them. Hair was ducktails (long upswept hair in the shape of a ducktail) or burr depending on which parent demanded a short haircut.

We made our way to the top of the mountain for an hour long dance session to twist and turn to the likes of Elvis Presley, Bobby Darin, Paul Anka, Ricky Nelson, Buddy Holly, the Everly Brothers, Fats Domino, Bill Haley and the Comets, Chuck Berry, Jerry Lee Lewis, and a host of other greats. We had the time of our life until the studio closed and moved to Fort Smith to their location on Fifth Street.

When we found out KFSA would continue Teen Town, we'd hop the old, white Twin City bus on Broadway, pay our ten cents and travel across the river. A scheduled stop, on Garrison Avenue, was about one block from the station and when it was time to go home the bus driver always waited a few minutes to make sure we got back on board. He'd smile, ask if we had fun and whistled, *That's All Right, Momma,* Elvis Presley's, Sun Record hit. We knew he was young at heart or had teenagers at home.

Both KFSA stations are gone, replaced with houses on Mount Vista and a vacant lot in Fort Smith where the station was housed. Teen Town is but a memory and some of the great artists are no longer with us. The songs won't go away ... they are alive and well in the hearts and minds of the 50's generation.

Joyce L. Rapier

PAPER DRIVES

The other day I was conversing with friends, Stanley Clark and Larry Gregory, at the Van Buren Fire Department. To teach children the fundamentals of safety, a fire prevention week is held in October, a month into the school year. The Van Buren Fire Department is astute in their teachings to young children as well as adults. This year, October 5th through the 11th, is the week set aside for their programs. He was saying how prevention should be adhered to everyday in maintaining fire alarms (changing batteries) and having an escape route in case of a fire. Keeping clutter to a minimum and away from any source of ignition will also help. Playing with matches, cigarette lighters and lighted candles are a major source for fires. Cleaning chimneys on a regular basis before the first cold spell will also help prevent a chimney fire. Fires can be deadly and destroy everything. Anything we can to do prevent them will bring peace of mind.

It's great that we have several fire department stations in Van Buren but in the 50's, our only fire department was one block from Sophia Meyer where the Municipal Complex stands today. The fire and police department complex was one small building but effective for the time. They did their jobs well and maintained safety but our population was not what it is today. In 2008, it would be in Van Buren's best interest to have more fire departments as the population is soaring.

Speaking to my friends brought to mind the popular paper drives back in the 50's. As a child Sophia Meyer's hallways seemed large and echoed with the footsteps of a teacher. We knew, if we were in the hallways during recess and got caught, a scolding was eminent. The echo of leather touching concrete was a sure fire way to made us scatter. However, during a paper drive, footsteps were muffled and so was the clanging of the usual loud fire alarms.

Hearing the reverberating clang from the bright red, round alarms, situated in various areas of the hallway, we knew a fire drill was at hand. Our routine was not to panic but to get out of our seats and lineup, putting one hand on the person's shoulder that was directly in front of us. In perfect form, all children walked safely but quickly out the egress. We were directed to stop at our allotted spot on the playground. The teachers did a head count to make sure everyone was out of the building. Sounding the all clear bell, students filed in queue back into the classroom.

Every school in our district, i.e., Sophia Meyer, King and Oak Grove, participated in a paper drive. Since I didn't remember the objective of the paper drive, whether the specific school got money or the grade who gathered the most paper got some type of reward, I phoned my school friend, Dayna. She couldn't remember, either, but we did have some laughs. Her comment was it was so long ago and mine to her was, "Don't say that because I like to think of it as a speck on the horizon."

Joyce L. Rapier

The paper drives were fun but as I look back upon the mounds of paper blocking the entryways ... deadly. We didn't think of harm but a fun way to have a contest. Dayna, the petite, raven haired beauty, and I, the white haired gangly girl, were allowed to venture to her house at 933 Main Street to collect her little Red Ryder wagon to haul paper back to the school. We couldn't remember if it was a fourth grade teacher, Mrs. Tull or Mrs. Davis, a fifth grade teacher, who gave us permission to roam down town Van Buren in search of bundled newspapers. In our quest to load the wagon to its capacity, we found (for shame) a risqué, picture laden, adult magazine. That's right ... one of those unclothed, here I am in all my glory, nudie magazines. We took a long look, stared at one another in disbelief at what we had seen and shoved it under the mound of papers. I have no idea whose hands got the magazine after we took it to school or if it was piled along with the other questionable material to be recycled.

The paper drive lasted several weeks. If the papers got wet from children coming in from rainy weather, the moldy scent would make a person sick. If you accidentally brushed against the newspapers, ink smudges adhered to hands or clothing. Before the paper drive was completed, only a narrow passage way was available to walk to our classrooms. As high as the ceiling, most of the twined bundles were stacked properly, while loose newspapers lay aimlessly on the floor.

Paper drives no longer exist except for curb side, recycle receptacles. It is a good thing our children and grandchildren are not given cart-blanche to go door to door or business to business to gather newspaper for school contests or projects. The best thing is that the Van Buren Fire Department is diligent in enforcing fire codes for schools and businesses and teaching students to be wise about fire safety. We should give thanks to the Van Buren Fire Department and its employees for helping us to be safe.

HAND ME DOWNS

What is it about used items? Some things might repulse us and others make us plow through musty buildings in search of the perfect item. Antique furniture can sit for years gathering patina or be marred with gouges from years past but when something catches our eye, it's a must have. Do we search out the best antique shops for the prize or are they tucked away in a family attic? Antiques are one of those things a lot of people covet, but the lowly "hand me down" clothing is frowned upon when mentioned. Why?

Growing up, "hand me downs" was a normal part of living. The old saying, "Use it up, wear it out, and make it do or do without", was a common formula for living. No one ever threw out clothing as the smaller child in the family would soon grow into it. If a family had several children, clothing could last for years. If torn, it might have been re-stitched in places or altered if it was too large. Boys' jeans were either cut off for shorts or made into skirts for little girls. Knee holes were patched with whatever was available and kids didn't think negative about wearing them. Maybe it was because their peers wore the same type of mended garments.

When things were too old and not fit for wearing, women would tear it into strips and weave them into homemade throw rugs. Quilts were made from the remaining pieces of material or stitched for dust cloths. Shoes were built to last and if they were too large for a sibling, a piece of cotton or material was stuffed into the toe. If they were too small for anyone in the family, a cousin or other relative received them. Nothing was discarded until it was so fragile it went into the cistern.

It doesn't bother me one iota to find a good buy in one of the consignment stores. Most of our area shops have quality clothing at a fraction of the cost a person would pay in a fashion conscious shop. Most people who consign clothing don't live in the same town, as they know to be seen in something someone else has worn, has a connotation to it. Clothing in a consignment store has been thoroughly cleaned and some items appear never worn. Perhaps something was purchased, worn one time and put aside. Maybe it was outgrown or they just didn't like it. Whatever reason, to pass up a good consignment shop because they sell only used clothing, is ludicrous. Yeah, I know ... kids today only want the new stuff and can't fathom being seen in something someone else has worn. It's a stigma or will warp their personalities. Hogwash! If there was a contest to win a jersey from a well known athlete or shoes from a favorite female star (worn one time) and the only rule was it would have to be worn by the winner, you can bet the winner would be wearing it to show their friends. They would be leaping for joy. Those items, whether they would like to admit it or not, would be considered "hand me downs."

Since we didn't have consignment shops in the 50's, churches would hold a rummage sale, coinciding with the first day of school. Rummage meant to pile things on a table, regardless of sizes and let the shopper sort through specific clothes. It was the norm to see entire families shopping and conversing with their friends as they sat down to eat free cookies, milk and coffee.

In the 60's, the round of shopping became garage sales from families wanting to pick up needed money. In the late 70's, clothing prices were reasonable as people became clothes horses and purchased from giant retailers. The 80's rolled around and good, quality, consignment shops were popping up all over the place from people getting rid of their purchasing whims of the 70's. A lot of people whose desire for new clothing saw higher interest rates and credit card explosions. It was getting out of control and they needed to find a source to save money. It was the consignment shops saving the day. In the 90's, a prosperous upswing saw more people at retail shops, but as usual, times have a way of pulling people back into reality. Once again, interest rates soared and people tightened their purse strings. Prices in clothing soared making people pull back from shopping sprees.

Nearly into 2009, we find ourselves holding on to the greenbacks in an attempt to thwart overspending. It is not only a local thing but an entire nation struggling to keep their heads above water. For people wanting to save money, but at the same time needing to provide clothing for their children, I do suggest consignment shops. One is located on Fayetteville Road in Van Buren. Another shop is located right across from the Frisco Depot. Fort Smith and Alma have tremendous avenues for the money conscious shopper, too. You can buy a lot of quality, name brand clothes for the price you might pay for one pair of jeans.

I do not own any consignment shops or am I affiliated with any but if you see me in one of them, I might say ... isn't this place great?

EASY OPEN PACKAGES

Do you remember when the simple task of opening a package was so easy, a flick of the fingernail would do the trick? Not so in this day and age. I believe it began around 1980 when some wacko decided to poison people when they swallowed a headache pill. Stupid, heinous twits! They had no clue what would transpire for those who have no desire to harm anyone.

Today, trying to open any type of package is like tunneling through a concrete barrier with a baby spoon. Even if a "stone worm" (got that little tidbit from a British comedy, Last of the Summer Wine), tried to chew its way through a package, it would give up in an instant. No wonder products cost a fortune. There are so many obstacles: boxes inside boxes, plastic inside plastic ... inside plastic, plastic inside boxes. Geesh, Louise ... cut down on the amount of packaging and reduce the price. Everything is running amok.

Have you ever tried to open a cereal insert? It appears to be made of Tyvek, a material used in making fishing license. You can't tear the stuff. You can't even rip it with a ten ton pair of pliers or destroy it by putting it in a garbage disposal. Well, I haven't tried the disposal, so it might be possible. Anyway, when you grit your teeth and your hands yank with all their might, cereal goes flying through the air and none of it lands in a bowl. It's too late for scissors ... crunch, crunch, crunch under foot ... hand me a broom.

Some products, if they are in boxes, are an additional security maze. You have to use a razor blade ... if you still have one of those little tin gadgets lying around the house. Those boxes might contain little bottles of medicine, aspirin, Beano, eye drops or nasal spray, and guess what ... they have corsets around the rim. Yeah, you read right, corsets. It's a band of plastic, glued down so tight; little women of the seventeenth century couldn't squirm out of it. She might burn it before she had to wear it again. Whew, two hurdles down and two more to go. Around the perimeter of the opening is ... you got it ... a thin layer of aluminum or plastic material. Take an ice pick to it. Open at last, or is it? Nope! Find those tweezers because you're going to need it to extract a six inch wad of cotton out of the bottle. Good grief, there may be ten little pills inside, so you best be taking them sparingly as the ordeal of opening another container will do you in.

Batteries! Those blasted battery cocoons are exasperating. It must have a layer of steel sandwiched or implanted in the plastic. It is almost impossible to puncture the secure case, especially when individual batteries are wrapped up like a papoose. If you jab the plastic container with a knife, you automatically run the risk of puncturing an artery or slicing off a finger. Somebody find me a chainsaw.

You would think the little woman of the twenty-first century would have a normal kitchen. Not so. She has to equip the cabinet or a drawer with power or hand tools. She needs in her ordinary, run of the mill kitchen ... a tweezers, pliers, hammer, screwdriver, wrench, awl, vise grips, anvil, blow torch, and chainsaw. Maybe even a jackhammer and a set of new false teeth in case her natural teeth have been gritted to the gums from exasperating attempts to open packages. In this day of miracle things, it's a miracle most women haven't gone off the deep end. We don't need a kitchen ... we need to live in a tool shop.

Yeah, I know it's a security thing (loss prevention for stores) and I am all for security when it comes to undermining or putting our lives in harm's way. Pills we take for life threatening diseases and some foods we consume, I understand the need for secure packaging. Come on, now, not everything needs to be cemented down with super glue or wedged inside a chain linked box. I sincerely hope authorities caught the insidious, caper pulling idiots who started this whole, mind boggling, insane, impossible to open packages stunt. It would be thrilling to know their sentence would be a life condemned to opening a ninety-thousand square foot warehouse, packed full of steel cased plastic packages with their teeth. Poetic justice is what it's called. It's bad enough to know our world is full of sociopaths and narcissistic lunatics, whose penchant to do us harm, is waiting, or lurking in the depths of lunacy to wrap our houses in a sixteen inch thick piece of plastic. When that happens, I'm out of here color me gone! I have had enough trouble trying to get cockeyed packages open. I don't want to be trapped on the inside of a power packaged house trying to get out ... I am not in hibernation.

Until it happens and I see someone, (best be smiling, you're on candid camera), wrapping my house with impenetrable plastic wrap, unhinge those cocooned batteries, put them in a brown paper bag, lower the price and give us all a break!

Joyce L. Rapier

LUNCH BUCKETS

Since 1900 most people have carried some kind of lunch bucket but it wasn't until the 1950's that the lunch box became a very marketable item. The most popular one for men was a black oval topped container holding a thermos. The handle was attached to triangular metal hinges and would lay flush to the top to keep it from snapping off the bucket. Inside the top, a glass lined coffee thermos was held firmly in place with a wire frame. Since the thermos was glass lined and didn't have the safety features thermoses have today, you had to be careful. If the liner accidentally broke, you might pour a cup of hot coffee full of glass slivers. Beneath the thermos was two areas defined for sandwiches and perhaps a slice of homemade pie or cake.

Daddy carried one of these lunch boxes everyday of his working life. Inside his lunch bucket was the normal hot coffee and a sandwich or two made of leftover meatloaf or hogshead cheese. The main thing he never forgot to pack inside his lunch bucket was a flashlight. The flashlight was high beamed and easy to fold into one of the lunch box slots. The light, attached to an elastic band, fit neatly around the top of his striped or dark blue railroad caps. It was needed as he walked the dark railroad yard. Those two items; lunch bucket and flashlight were life savers. The food was for consumption and the light was to give a broad band to night vision. Most of the time, daddy worked the graveyard shift and ate on the run or sat with the other workers in the small time shack near the round house. It was easier to sit among respective workers while consuming meals because there weren't too many drive through, slap it at me eateries close to his job. Van Buren had some great cafés but most Sunday church goers used the eateries as a special treat. People, working down town and close to the cafés, catered to them.

Over the years, I have accumulated various sorts of lunch boxes ... not buckets. I think my first two were Hopalong Cassidy and Roy Rogers / Dale Evans lunch boxes and I loved toting them around. I am not sure food was ever put inside them but I did put frogs and grasshoppers inside Hopalong Cassidy. I wanted to see if it would hop - a - long! Mother nearly had a coronary when she opened it. Insects and critters popped out at her. The grasshoppers ceased when one of them spit "tobacco juice" on me and bit the tip of my finger. Contrary to popular belief, those flying, leaf eating, head turning insects ... do bite. The frogs ceased when I was told I would get warts and prince charming wouldn't kiss me. I don't know what happened to my lunch boxes but I imagine they went to the great "file thirteen" or used as small tool holders for my dad. If truth was known, I probably buried them under the house along with old coins. I was bad about burying money because I didn't like to spend it.

When my kids (three of them) came along, we started off with plain, brown paper bags with sandwiches wrapped in wax paper. The kids hated the wax paper because if it came loose from the sandwich the bread became stale. Then they found lunch boxes and from 1965 to 1982 we ran the gamut of lunch boxes and plastic lunch bags. Each successive year, the kids thought they couldn't be seen with last year's choice, so those boxes would be scrunched to the back of the cabinet and three new ones would take their place. There were GI Joes, Batman, all kinds of Disney characters, Star Trek, Bruce Lee, plaid ones and plain ones. Those for little girls included: Barbie and Ken, Dr. Seuss, Snow White, Holly Hobbie, Bionic woman, and if you could name it, manufacturers made it. When the fad of carrying a lunch box faded, and my kids thought they were too old to be seen with one, I had amassed so many my cabinets tilted. In fact, some of them were mangled or crayoned so bad, I couldn't figure out whether they were the original I purchased or something the kids swapped. Hello attic.

Soon, the lunch box went by the wayside and the contraption of the day turned into hot or cold, small, thermos containers. They were large enough for soup or maybe a dollop of blackberry cobbler. Some could be placed in the freezer and used to make Icees or ice cream. Those, too, became passé when they chose to eat food from the cafeteria in school.

It's good I don't have the need to purchase any more metal or plastic food carriers or sandwich bags because my attic can't house one more discarded lunch box. Maybe the magic fairy will come along, zap them with her wand and transport everything to the kids' attic. I don't intend to hold my breath.

Perhaps Antiques Road Show will show up in our little town and I can have the opportunity to sell them to the highest bidder and retire. I'm sure they would laugh, tell me they were mass produced, aren't antique and I would be better off burying them in the backyard. I guess I'd better fetch a shovel, hire a jackhammer to whittle through the rocks and get busy before I am an antique.

BEST FRIENDS

Oh, mighty mirror on the wall, why have you cast this aging spell ... upon everyone ... large and small? When you look in a mirror, what do you see? Is another wrinkle creeping around the mouth, or do you hear the caw of the crow as it etches its claws deeper into the corners of the eyes? My thoughts are that a body is like a time capsule. I see it as bone, sinew and feelings, encased in a tightly woven mask of skin, twirling with each successive second, minute, hour, day and decade. Each rotation loosens a tad, till we no longer reflect or see the person we were the first time we looked in a mirror.

We lose sight of those things we dreamed of as a child and pages of life flip in mach speed. We aren't given guarantees when we are born and we do not come with a use by date stamped on our foreheads. There is no magic cure all to stave off aging as each of us trod through the process of growing older. The only thing guaranteed for each of us, if we live long enough, is birth, taxes and death. Those things in order are a given.

Like all childhood friends we declared to never forget each other. We would always be in touch but ... would we? Unfortunately, time has a way of pulling friends apart by different interests. Marriages, growing families, moving to another state and a host of other things declare its state of fact. Growing apart is not an intended thing but it happens. One stable thought is we were always friends ... going separate ways with different directions of purpose. She and I put our families first knowing they were the most precious things on earth.

It seems like yesterday we met and the memories flood over me like a waterfall. She was born on the nineteenth day and so was I. While several months apart in age, we laughed and celebrated our birthdays together. Our thoughts were that we were meant to be best friends because day nineteen was special ... it had to be ... or we would have never met. We vowed our friendship by being "blood sisters." We cringed as we pricked our fingers with a huge darning needle and pressed our bleeding fingers together ... securing a lifelong friendship. It was.

She could laugh the hardest of any person I ever knew, but at the same time, stop in mid stream and stare me in the eye. Without warning the laughter would resume. It was hysterical at times because we never knew why we were laughing. As a young girl, she could be a force to reckon with when confronted and could put a person in their place if need be ... but not for long because of her gentle, patient nature. Her deep blue eyes softened when watching a butterfly float on a breeze, and her gentle touch caressed a wounded soul. Like all little kids, she was complicated ... but, then again ... what child isn't?

Sometimes shy and reserved, she would twist the strands of her long black hair as if to say, "Wait a minute till I size you up ... then we'll talk." As she grew with confidence, it didn't take her long to be relaxed in the presence of a stranger or be friendly and accommodating to those less fortunate. She was giving and straightforward and knew which direction her life would go. One thing I will never forget is her love for iced tea and the way we clinked glasses together in a toast to best friends.

Things held in my mind are gathering eggs in a chicken house and being swarmed by mites. She would scratch my back and I hers. Our appreciation and respect for each other was reciprocal without strings attached. Sleeping in a tent on a hot summer night while waiting for the mosquitoes to devour us and screaming when her brothers whacked the tent. We said "fix-fix" when something in our make believe world was broken. We waited up till midnight to watch a flower, the Night Blooming Cereus, unfold its beauty. Putting on stage shows for our friends and families and stomping through mud in a pair of twenty-five cent cowboy boots. So many things transpired in our world, it would take an entire book to fill.

My best friend and childhood confident is gone but only in the physical sense. This is not part of our make believe world and we can't "fix-fix" this break in departure. The time capsule, encasing my friend, gave way to bigger and better things beyond. She leaves a host of friends and a combined family she adored. Although she is walking over a bridge to see a glorious rainbow of promises and sitting among the angels, I know in my heart, one day I will see her twist the strand of hair.

Until we meet again, RIP ... Geraldine Beth (Jeri Beth) Epperson. February 19, 1945 - September

22, 2008. You are gone but not forgotten as we are "blood sisters" forever.

Joyce L. Rapier

SALT PORK AND HOMEMADE BISCUITS

Some of you will cringe at the thought of eating salt pork bacon but it is one of the tastiest pieces of bacon you could ever hope to eat. Add a slice or two to a homemade biscuit and it is lip smacking good.

When Grandma and Grandpa Hawkins moved from Frog Holler, they lived, many years ago, in one of the row houses where the Crawford County Jail is located. Then they moved to the northern most part of Knox Street. They raised hogs on the east slope of their property and I delighted in seeing the little piglets. One of the old sows was a grumpy old sort and hell bent for leather to run me into the ground if I dared set one foot inside her domain. She didn't know that when those little piglets got large enough to fend for themselves, she was a gone gosling ... and I don't mean goose! It was none too soon for me to see the old sow depart this earth, but to tell the truth, I was nowhere to be found when it was time for butchering. No, I never heard a pig screaming bloody murder as Grandma knew how to eliminate those sounds. In those times, it was eat hog or die and a way of life. When it was butchering time, we all went to their house to help because it was more than a two people procedure. It was a disgusting sight but I learned a great deal about how they managed to survive with what they had. When it was over, I didn't mind helping with whatever needed to be done. They cured hams, bacon, and made hogshead cheese from all the leftover meat. Trimming the rind to a fine sliver, cracklings were deep fried for snacks or added to cornbread.

On the south side of their house was a small smoke house and the butchered meat would be hung inside the smoke belching apparatus to cure. It would take all day and half the night. They soaked apple wood from their apple trees to get the best flavor with a few chunks of hickory thrown in for good measure. On occasion, the smoke house would catch fire and a bucket brigade (no water hoses) handled the situation. When the meats were golden brown, they were wrapped in some kind of cloth and stored in a cold cellar beneath the house, because, even though they had electricity, they didn't have a freezer.

For the salt pork, Grandma would mix a concoction of spices and salt and put the partially smoked pork down inside the brine. All of this was done in her kitchen and periodically, she would check the meat. The brine was discarded and then the she would start the process all over again. I don't know how many times she did it as I got bored and went outside to play. When it was time to salt the pork, all hands were on deck. A massive cloth was put on the kitchen table and cure all salt was poured generously atop it. Each piece of meat was rolled and pounded until it looked like a giant wad of white powder. They were then tied into bundles of cheese cloth and hung in the cellar to complete its cure. She must have known what she was doing because none of us ever got sick from eating contaminated food. I wouldn't attempt to do any of these procedures but I do make summer sausage from ground beef and freeze it for the winter.

Grandma's homemade biscuits were yummy. She used lard rendered from the hog as lard from a store was too expensive. She would pour flour into a large bowl (she never measured anything) and add some salt. Baking powder and baking soda came in a box (smaller than a small cereal box) and she used a cup to scoop out the right amount. The dried ingredients were swirled about with her hands to mix thoroughly and then the lard was gently folded into the contents with buttermilk added last. Everything was folded not stirred. Pressing the dough with her hands, she rolled the dough to about an inch thick. She cut each round of biscuit with a piece of tin cut from a large can. When those biscuits were cooking, the aroma was pure heaven.

While she was preparing the biscuits; sliced salt pork was being boiled to remove the salt. It was done several times to extract excess salt from the exterior of the bacon and then the salt water was used as a weed killer. Patted to dry, the bacon was put inside the oven to cook while the biscuits rested atop the stove to stay warm. It was a feast to slice into a biscuit, put homemade butter inside the steaming golden topped bread and then put slabs of salt pork inside.

When Grandma and Grandpa moved back to town, all those activities ceased. No more butchering or smoke houses existed because times were changing. They needed to be near medical facilities to make living easier for old tired hands. The only thing that didn't change was Grandma's biscuits and salt pork. She was able to find small slabs of it in her local grocery store and continued to cook it for all the grandkids. It didn't taste quite like Grandma's homemade salt pork but with a little imagination, transported us back in time.

Grandma's ninety-eight years of generous nature and know how left all her grandkids with a legacy of timeless thoughts and place to remember.

Recipe for summer sausage:

You can alter this recipe with the spices. Do not alter the ground beef or curing salt.

* 5 pounds ground beef

- 5 teaspoons curing salt
- 1/2 cup mustard seed
- 6 tablespoons garlic powder (I like it real garlicky)
- 2 teaspoon cayenne pepper   (I like it hot!)
- 1 tablespoon red pepper flakes
- 1 tablespoon salt
- 1 teaspoon hickory-flavored liquid smoke

1. In a large bowl, mix beef, curing salt, mustard seed, garlic powder, cayenne, red pepper flakes, salt, and liquid smoke. Cover with plastic, and refrigerate for three days, mixing well once a day.
2. On the fourth day, preheat oven to 200 degrees F (100 degrees C).
3. Shape the mixture into five logs, and place on a wire rack over a large drip pan. Bake for eight hours, and then remove to cool on paper

towels. Let cool, then wrap logs individually in plastic wrap. Chill completely before slicing. They also freeze well.

HALLOWEEN

Main Street in Van Buren was a hub of activity in October. Two weeks before Halloween all the merchants displayed grand decorations around the large portals. The windows were spectacular. They were bedecked with cauldrons spewing dry ice, brooms, ceramic or plastic black cats, angel hair with spiders and crows hanging from the ceiling and an occasional witch flew from a long wire. Orange and black crepe paper secured with push pins dangled from the interior ceilings. Gray moss-covered tombstones engraved with eerie RIP angled in corners, bales of straw might have fake hands jutting from them, pumpkins carved with spooky expressions, and scarecrows (sometimes live people) amid stacks of tall, brown corn stalks greeted every passerby. It was a sight to behold and a captivating experience for little kids. Imaginations ran rampant.

Inside the five and dime stores, all kinds of noise makers could be found. Blow ticklers, bright orange and black ratchets, whistles, horns, clackers and a host of other items fancied our persuasion. The graphics on all of the noise makers was remarkable. Usually made of tin, some of them twirled when you cranked the handle. Others were made like a paddle where the small wooden ball clanked against metal. Some were made into a kaleidoscope where witches mysteriously but animatedly appeared when the cylinder was rotated. Bags of sweet paraffin whistles, candy corn, licorice sticks and other enticing goodies made our mouths salivate. Masks ... those you might see at a Mardi Gras ... were plain or elegantly adorned with feathers or rhinestones. They came in various colors to match the attire someone would wear to an upscale party. A few kids' costumes could be bought but they were made out of thin material or plastic and ripped apart at the seams. Most of us opted for wearing our own clothes or over sized adult clothing and modifying our faces so we couldn't be recognized. We might dress up like a clown, witch, or zombie but who could take a seven year old zombie seriously when he/she giggled saying Trick or Treat?

We didn't fear the dark on Halloween because four or five kids (ages seven to fifteen in groups) walked all over the neighborhood. Those who could afford candy had a porch light on and those without a light we didn't visit. Some adult homeowners would wait outside their front door and shine a flashlight to make sure we didn't fall in a ditch. Most kids didn't have an orange pumpkin to house their goodies. Instead, we glued a handle on a brown grocery bag, decorated the sack with bright colored crayon drawings and set out on a fun filled night. Half the time the sack would burst open and kids would scramble to pick up the lost bounty.

I only remember having a couple of very special Halloweens. The neighborhood kids tricked and treated before it got dark so we could go with our parents to Van Buren's main street for a Mardi Gras. If I remember correctly, the gala event didn't start until around eight-thirty in the evening. It seemed as though every citizen of Van Buren and perhaps people from Fort Smith filled the lower portion of Main Street to celebrate Halloween.

Bright colored beads dangled around our necks mimicking the ever popular Mardi Gras in New Orleans. Donned in grand costumes, the adults were mask faced and gathered to enjoy festivities. Some of them were dressed in the era of the early 1900's or Harlequin and others in the 1920's garb. I remember seeing one broad shouldered man with a wide tie, fedora and spats. The spats fascinated me because of the white band circling the shoe. The cigar he smoked nearly gagged me to death while I stood there in awe looking at his captivating stance. He reminded me of a gangster I saw in a Dick Tracy comic strip. A secret Mr. and Mrs. mingled throughout the crowd and the objective was to find them before another person screamed out their names. The kids bobbed for apples, played games and collected candy handed out by a jester. It was absolutely marvelous and everyone had fun. No alcohol was permitted although I am sure there were those persons who couldn't resist getting schnockered, bleary eyed and obnoxious.

All too soon the evening was over and we walked back home talking about the fun we had. It wasn't like it is today where parents have to inspect candy before an eager child consumes it. No one thought of Halloween in a bad light or that it was a sinister activity. Celebrating Halloween has been around for centuries in honor of the dearly departed (saints) and the church sanctified it as All Saints Day.

As I reminiscence a golden era of my youth and visit the store fronts in pictures of my mind, I wish all of you a hauntingly, "BOO"tiful Halloween.

Source:
http://www.history.com/minisites/Halloween

THANKSGIVING

Every year, as far back as I can remember, we went to Grandma's house for Thanksgiving. Aunts, uncles, cousins, nephews, nieces and friends were invited because it was the time of year to give thanks for all we had and to share the food we prepared.

Grandma's house was small and I do mean small! Walking in the front door meant being hit full force with heat exuding from the space heater. Body temperatures, along with the space heater, made the inside thermometer close to 112 degrees. It wasn't hot ... it was blistering. Coats would be jerked off and flung in the small bedroom with everyone saying they were hotter than a two dollar pistol. The poor bed swayed in the middle with mounds of coats, sweaters and caps.

The round kitchen table with a white table cloth was situated in front of a window. A bench, large enough for four small kids or two adults to sit, was behind the table. Most times the bench would shift with too heavy an adult and the kids would rise in the air. It was comical and animated to see forks extracted from a piece of turkey or watch as someone sat down on a plate of uneaten food. Cranberry sauce is terrible on white clothing.

Food of all kinds bedecked the table leaving little space to place a plate. Heaven forbid if we tried to eat at the table ... it didn't happen but no one cared. We stood, went outside or sat in the living room ... if there was a place to sit. Most times a ballgame was on television and between munches and screaming at a player, it wasn't the place to be. We would maneuver back to the kitchen but it was precarious, as other bodies had to be gently persuaded to move out of the line of fire ... bodies to bodies with full plates ready to be pushed into a lap or dropped on top of a head.

We would be so full of food; we wobbled and then went back for more. Sometimes we would move to the backyard to play a little football or games with the kids and pick up pecans having dropped from the massive pecan trees. We couldn't resist cracking open the paper shell goodies to munch on the sweet meats. Gorged to the max, swearing off food for a week because buttons were popping ... where could you find us? In the kitchen picking at food because it was there. The one food no one ever tired was Grandma's vanilla cream pie with chocolate swirl ... eight of them in total but never enough to satiate our appetites. They were not ordinary pies ... they literally melted in the mouth. The pie crust was amazingly flaky, always firm and crisp on the bottom and fluted around the edges. The filling was not store bought but made from scratch. The vanilla cream, smooth on the tongue dissolved in haste, like butter on a hot, steaming biscuit. Chocolate, swirled atop the pie, complimented the gourmet dessert.

Grandma got smart and started using paper plates and plastic cups because her small sink, overloaded to capacity with every dirty dish known to man, made everyone cringe. When someone began washing (no dishwasher) it invariably turned into a free-for-all suds fight. What amazed me was it took two hours to cook something, thirteen minutes to consume the delectable repast, two seconds to fill the sink and six hours to wash everything. There was something wrong with that picture!

Most of the leftovers were divided into small portions and taken home by all of us. However, we always had several plates fixed for other people who were hungry. Since Grandma lived close to the Missouri Pacific Railroad tracks, we would take plates full of goodies to hobos walking the tracks. Sometimes they were taken aback or embarrassed by what we were offering, so we put the plates and plastic utensils on a table (Grandma put it there for this purpose) and walked away. The food always disappeared and the plates were put in a paper sack receptacle. It was a nice feeling to know our Thanksgiving meal touched so many lives.

As Grandma grew older, the group got larger. It included grandchildren and great-grandchildren. Forever afraid it would be Grandma's last Thanksgiving, the little house rocked with more and more people. Then the inevitable happened, Grandma became too fragile to devote time and effort to a big get together. We all had to make our own family traditions and she never missed an opportunity to be at someone else's house. It was her turn to sit back and relax.

The little house that was, was sold and Grandma was no more. Grandma lived to be ninety-eight years young, and if she could, she would be cranking out vanilla cream pies and feeding the hobos. Thanks for the memories, Grandma.

SCHOOL CARNIVALS

It was six-thirty in the evening as Jeri Beth and I clasped hands and tiptoed by Ocker Funeral Home. The sun had dropped off the edge of the western skies making the atmosphere crisp and scary. To our right, a black hearse was parked in the narrow driveway on Seventh Street. One light was glaring downward at an entryway. Shadows lurched as tree limbs swayed in the breeze and a few wayward autumn leaves swirled at our feet. Our faces were pensive as to what might jump out at us.

After all, it was Friday, a very ominous Friday, four days before Halloween and spooks and goblins were swarming in our minds, threatening to teem in front of unsuspecting carnival goers. Street lights, very far apart, seemed to echo danger lurking in our paths. We could swear we saw bats swooping down toward our heads and wondered if they were vampires wanting to puncture our necks. Would Dracula miraculously appear, caped in his black attire with fanged mouth, eager to devour our souls? Would zombies, draped in ragged, dirty clothing in their escape from the tomb, progress toward us?

Hearts pounding at the speed of light, we raced across Broadway in search of friendly faces. One and a half block to go before we reached our destination and we were panicked–panicked, I tell you. It might have been a cool evening but our clothes were drenched with hot sweat. This was just the beginning of a Friday full of terror and what, pray tell, would we encounter when we entered Sophia Meyer School?

The hallways were swarming with children and adults, some dressed in costumes and others in their normal attire. Behind each closed classroom door, we couldn't fathom why it was so mysterious. Was it a plot by the teachers or the PTA (Parent Teacher Association) to keep us in suspense or were they eager to lock us up in a vacuum of dark terror? Sinister laughter from adults emanated from every nook and cranny while goose bumps shot up the spine with every child screaming bloody murder. Only a few children at a time were allowed to enter the rooms to view the victimizing arena and sworn to secrecy when they exited. How the adults managed to keep the kids from telling the secret of the room, I do not know, but the kids zipped their lips. An offered piece of candy would not entice them to reveal the secrets behind closed doors.

Nothing was disappointing in each of the rooms. Something was there for every child, whether they were grade school students or siblings too young to attend. First grade had fishing poles with bobbers attached to the end of the line. Each child took a turn to see what could be caught. A makeshift wall, decorated with enormous whales, small fishes and other sea creatures, was near the blackboard. It provided an area to cast the line in search of the elusive bag of goodies hiding somewhere within its boundary. When the adult behind the wall wrapped the bobber around the bag of goodies, we knew we hit the jackpot or "fish" of the evening. All kinds of candy and trinkets, donated by area merchants, were secreted in our prize catch.

Some rooms had sock hops. We took off our shoes and waited patiently for our turn to maneuver the obstacle at hand. It was a giant hop scotch. Numbered blocks were special because landing on them meant you were given a pair of socks donated by W.B. Smith. I don't remember any child not coming out of the room without a pair of white socks.

Cake walks were in a couple of rooms (parents made the cakes) and it was hard to win one of them. When the music stopped, if your feet weren't on the designated number drawn by the announcer, you went out of the room empty handed. Small pillow tosses (bean bags) were in another room to win pencils, crayons and ruled paper.

My all time favorite rooms were the spook house and dungeon, put on by the fifth and six grades. In the spook house, a black light was used magnifying the horrors surrounding ghastly drawings. Adults dressed up as witches, ghosts and other horrifying creatures lunged at children with grimacing faces. The dungeon was the last room to visit on the night of horrors. We were blind folded and led through a maze of spider webs (angel hair), cold air exuding from a cauldron of dry ice, and were told to run our fingers through icy cold, supposed brain matter. Parts of it (peeled grapes and cooked spaghetti) were gooey, marble sized, stringy and disgusting. To exit the room, a wobbly platform on some kind of rollers with air shooting from beneath it, made you feel as though you were hovering in space without a parachute.

All too soon, the school event was over. The carnival we anticipated and enjoyed was a memory to fill our minds till the next Halloween. However, the evening wasn't over ... it was just beginning! Pitch black outside, grotesque mind games, no street lights ... Ocker Funeral Home, hearses, bats, Dracula and Zombies! Run ... feet ... run!

CHRISTMAS PAST

In Charles Dickens' 1843 novel, *A Christmas Carol*, Ebenezer Scrooge, the protagonist, and antanonist, is hard boiled, domineering and despises Christmas. Bob Cratchit, the clerk in the Scrooge business, is met with distaste and shabby treatment. Giving Cratchit a day off for Christmas with pay is certainly not what Scrooge wants to do because he sees it as a gouge to his pocketbook. Ghosts shatter Scrooge with past, present and future clips of his behavior to fellow men. They show him how bah humbug, selfish attitudes create inward problems and unless he changes a path of self destruction, he will grow to hate himself. He can stay in a world of darkness or see the world in a new light with love surrounding him.

Childhood innocence doesn't regard Mr. Scrooge as someone to embrace nor does a child want to think of such things. Children are oblivious to the bah humbug side of life because of the gentle nature they possess. When I was a child, Scrooge didn't exist as I wasn't aware of anything but what my eyes saw. It was a time for happiness as I searched the night skies for the magi's North Star, wondering how they could possibly travel so far in search of the Baby Jesus. At the same time, knowing the birth of Jesus was why we celebrated Christmas, it was also a time for wonderment, a time for the elusive Santa Claus.

In my mind, Baby Jesus and Santa were related in a strange sort of way. Both of them were full of love, giving and harbored no resentment to anyone. It was a time to rejoice, a time to cry and above all else, a time to remember ... remember the sights, smells, sometimes snow, and hot chocolate and twinkling lights.

In our house, the Christmas tree was a symbol of good times to follow. I was anxious to search the tree for an abandoned birds nest so I could place a plastic Cardinal within its twigs. The nest was a sign of birth, a rite of passage. A bright, silver star adorned the top with homemade paper ropes draping the cedar fronds. Popcorn strings made the whole room aromatic while a few bubbling, electric candle lights flickered. Red and green glass bulbs dangled while competing with silver icicles. There wasn't gold, frankincense or myrrh under our tree and no presents. It was simple. A red mesh bag full of apples, oranges and nuts was what I enjoyed most but I wouldn't get those until Santa appeared. My mouth watered as nothing smelled better than crisp fresh fruit. Any presents we might receive wouldn't be seen till Santa arrived on Christmas Eve.

Yes, we did have Santa Claus ... a real, live, jolly, red suited, white bearded ... ho, ho, hoing Santa Claus. It was one of the most wonderful sights I ever saw with he in the wide, black buckled belt with toy filled, rope drawn brown sack slung over his shoulder. It wasn't a figment of my imagination or a blink of the eye of a hope filled child's dream. He was real! He went to every house in the neighborhood on Henry Street and some of the surrounding streets ... especially if small children lived there. I found out later, all the parents had to do was phone 711W.

Around six in the evening, my daddy always disappeared and it upset me to no end. I kept telling him he would miss Santa but he never listened to me. Even my pleas of telling him Santa only comes on Jesus' birthday, the best time of the year ... he would smile a silly little smile and pat me on the head. He always said, "If I see Santa, I'll make sure he doesn't pass up 212 Henry Street. I'll tell him to call 711W if he's going to be late." Off he went into the night and I was sad. I cried but my tears dried up as I figured he had to go to work. Little did I know that his work was more than hard labor! It was a gift of love, a meaningful, single night's work filling the hearts and minds of wide eyed children.

Promptly, at nine-thirty in the evening, a robust ho, ho, ho and a pound on the door sent shivers up my spine. It was time ... time to see the jolly old man whose appearance was thought of as a fantasy. Mother was standing behind me because on the very first visit, I bolted and didn't want anything to do with Santa. He scared the beejeebers out of me, so Mother, on consecutive visits, made sure I didn't come unhinged. This Christmas Eve as I sat on his lap, I could smell a faint aroma of Old Spice cologne. It was so familiar and the steel, gray eyes peering down at me made me melt. Was it? I wasn't sure if it was Santa or Daddy inside that bright red suit handing me presents but I knew I was happy. I didn't care because no one could make me not believe in Santa Claus ... he was there, inside my house listing all the "not so nice things" I had done during the year but adding with a hug, all the good things.

As I grew older, the secret was revealed as I saw the wedding band on the left hand of Santa. It was my Daddy's wedding band, the one I twisted around on his finger when he held my hand and I commented to Santa about my Daddy's ring. He said, "Mrs. Claus should have reminded me to take it off and he might not be able to make it next Christmas as the old red suit had run its course." I hugged his neck and said, "I understand."

Of all the memories, this one stands infinity. Yes, there is a Santa Claus and he lived with me and made a lot of little children happy. Thanks, Daddy ... uh, Santa Claus.

OUR CHARLIE BROWN CHRISTMAS

Many years after Santa Claus put away the red suit and white beard, Christmas didn't change. It was still the simple life, but years had a way of moving me in a different direction. A marriage, children and grandchildren took the spotlight as I drifted a world away from twisting the ring on my Daddy's finger ... Santa Claus' finger.

My husband, Dan, and I began our own traditions. Our first Christmas away from family and friends consisted of living with meager funds. Wingo Hall, a married students apartment complex on the campus of ASTC (Arkansas State Teachers College) in Conway, was filled with families just like us ... struggling to make ends meet while paying tuition. With all the hubbub of activities, studying and learning to cope with each other on a one to one basis, we vowed to make Christmas a simple time. Would it last?

We hadn't managed to accumulate material things as the apartment had all the necessary furnishings to get us through the hump of college life. It was a whirlwind of juggling everyday necessities, a struggle worthwhile to find our niche in life. We managed on a shoestring of money and a lot of faith. I would not change one thing as it cemented our path.

Our first Christmas was a Charlie Brown Christmas. Finding a Christmas tree was like maneuvering through a maze of scavenger hunts ... look here, look there, pick, poke and grab the leftovers. It was delightful but left us exhausted. On a whim, we decided to select the most awful tree. It was nothing more than the top of a whacked up pine but it would be the perfect little tree for our small area. Not more than two feet tall, the limbs appeared sickly as an emaciated, starved budgie. With a little bit of tender loving care, it turned into the most beautiful tree we dared hope to find. At a discount store in Conway, the money we spent ate into our grocery funds but we bought a few glass bulbs, a package of tinsel and a forty-nine cent, gold, plastic star. It was the shopping spree to last a life time because the little tree stood proud. When the morning sun shined through the window, the star cast a hue of brilliant colors. It was as though the tree had a life of its own, defying the axe. Two little presents were under the tree. It was glorious.

As we had more children, it was a time of anxiety. It was stressful to find the right presents, to dart hither, thither and yon to satisfy everyone wanting to see the kids. We understood but the children didn't. They wanted to stay home to enjoy the few gifts they received. After several years of exasperating treks, we decided the traditions for our family would be one of simplicity. The visits to family would be before Christmas and it solved a great problem for everyone. The stress was relieved for us, as well as our parents.

When Christmas became too commercial and we realized buying presents was another major cause of stress, Dan and I made an additional vow ... no more presents for each other. If we wanted, we could celebrate Christmas at other times of the year and enjoy Christmas day as it should be ... quiet, restrained and full of promise. We stopped searching for wacky gifts for our parents. Throughout the year, our presents to them would consist of paying utility bills, a gift certificate for a meal or meals at our house, stationery for those who liked to write letters, a bag of birdseed for their feathered friends (one of my favorite pastimes), a bag of fruit, a card with a letter enclosed about a nostalgic time or what they meant to us, or groceries. They were staples and things from the heart and not another whatnot to dust.

Now that our children are grown and we have grandchildren, we buy "Santa's deliveries" for the wee ones and "hang" our children's gifts on the tree. Our children understand the necessity to have their own traditions, are not pressured to be at our beck and call and have been told not to give us gifts ... we want nothing but their happiness. There is no demand, no pressure and no anxiety. It's the way it should be as they learn to relax and enjoy the season ... to visit because they want to without expectations.

We have had the glittering lights studding our shrubs and trees. They were beautiful but they couldn't compete with simplistic beauty ... a single, guiding North Star in the night's sky. For me, every evening is Christmas as all I have to do is to look up and see the strands of brilliant lights encompassing the earth. It is surreal with form ... a masterpiece. As for gifts, ours are free and are best ... a smile, hug, encouragement, listening to Christmas carols, sitting down to a Christmas meal and being with one another. We always have a tree ... a simple, non pretentious tree and for forty-seven years Dan has placed the forty-nine cent, little gold star upon its top. It still reflects, in shining glory prisms, the Charlie Brown Christmas we had so many years ago.

My present to all of you is one of purity, peace, joy and happiness. Merry Christmas to all, and to all ... a good night.

NEW YEAR

My favorite saying is "I go to sleep in January and wake up in December." It was something daddy always said when a New Year was barreling down, running amok as if the world would spin out of control if it couldn't get here on time.

It seems like yesterday when we celebrated the New Year on our front lawn. For me, the year dragged its feet as it hung in school days and zipped by on summer vacation. It couldn't make up its mind. It was a push me pull you kind of occurrence. On one hand, I loved seeing a New Year peek its head into December screaming for all of us to hurry up and enjoy a brand new season. Then again, all the things I enjoyed in the present year were nothing more than fleeting memories. I couldn't go back to experience what I left behind. It would be a new beginning of sights, smells and one of a kind happening. No New Year, past, present or future will be exactly the same because

Mother Nature colors shades of gray in our hair, puts a wrinkle here and there and tells us it's time to move on toward our destination.

I never understood why mother cried as the ominous twelve bells pealed out, "It's gone!" Was it ominous? At the time, yes, but I didn't make the connection until many years later. While mother reloaded the double barreled shotguns, daddy aimed a shotgun full of birdshot into the air and pulled the trigger. With each successive bong of the clock and hearing the repercussions of twelve shots, cold chills engulfed me. Uncertain if the cold, outside air was causing Goosebumps to pickle my flesh or the fear of a New Year invading my mother's space couldn't be digested. I knew it was a celebration of sorts, but somehow, I wondered if daddy was trying to thwart the New Year from entering their own private world. When the gunshots ceased, they stood embraced, in the quiet of the night hugging my sister and me so tight I thought we would burst. A kiss on the foreheads, we were shooed inside the house. It was already the New Year.

Such as it is now, many New Years have passed our threshold and I do understand why mother cried. Not so sad that the years quickly faded into the sunset but wondering what the New Year would bring. Like mother and daddy, we have seen the good times and bad times and all the in between. Nothing, though, is new under the sun and history repeats itself. Even new birth of spring is the same as we watch impatiently for the first red breasted robin. Flowers pop into view, trees leaf forth in splendor and once again months zip by with each rotating day. We are all cycles of nature's change and no matter what we say or do will dissuade the master course.

Some of us enjoy festivities of counting down the minutes as the ball drops at Times Square. Others go to gala parties, listen, and watch or set off fireworks to celebrate a joyful time and some swear by New Year's resolutions. I don't stay awake for the New Year like I have done in the past (too sleepy), won't fire a shotgun in the air like my daddy did in bygone years (psst, it's illegal), but I might cry thinking about the nostalgic, wonderful milestones crossing my path. One thing I will not do is make New Year's resolutions. Been there, done that and I find it's best to be true to myself. So, I resolve not to resolve, it makes a fool of me. For what I say that I will do, I know I won't, you see! Those are the last two lines of a poem, Resolve Not, I wrote in 1987.

Here is a little poem I wrote to remind me why December is so important (sometimes it's best to be last), and why the New Year is so eager to come forth in always wanting to be first.

December Rules the Cast © 2006 Joyce Rapier

The Master swings the pendulum while in his captain's seat.
His table's round, twelve seats are found, in one to twelve countdowns.
December reins the well known group; he's the leader of the troupe.
Each calendar page is pulled from stays ... the staples lose their grip.
You wonder why December rules; he's last in journey's trip.
Cause, one by one, months fall from grace and December's still in place.
Until the hand ticks off the time; the last minute rules in kind.
Then the Master swings again ... the pendulum comes full round.
Another year finds time to bring twelve months they will be found.
Then again we once will pull twelve pages from the past

To find another year is gone and December ruled the cast.

May all of you have a great and prosperous New Year 2009 and while you are playing arm chair quarterback, reading a good book or corralling young kids ... don't forget to eat those black-eye peas, cornbread, greens and hog jowls.

PENNY CANDY

Do you remember penny and sometimes two for a penny candy? Yes, there was such a thing and penny candies were large. They weren't like candy of today, a dollop one bite; give me $1.25 for a scent of what used to be. At our local grocer, Matlock's Grocery Store, on Lafayette Street, all you had to do was drop your penny on the counter and select from the yummiest delectable candies ever.

Guy and Jewell Matlock ran a grocery store, one block from my house. At the time, it didn't appear to be a block away but several blocks when short legs were counting paces while stumbling over rocks in the road. If it was muddy or icy outside, look out Charlie, because one slip of the foot sent you spiraling down the road...post haste. I didn't have time to look to see if my body was following me as I was too busy wondering how many bruises would appear on my backside. Believe me, I had more than I dared count but it was worth the effort to peer inside the candy trove. I wondered if I turned sideways, would someone think of me as a bowl of black and blue chocolate pudding. Black from the bruises and mud covered clothing, or blue from the icy inclement weather, whatever the case may be, I was uncertain if it was me in the body I wore.

Chocolates were never my favorite unless it covered a passel of peanuts or heath bars. It was the crunchy tidbits inside the dark coated chocolate tempting my taste buds. Chocolate was messy and left a tell tale sign, whereas the brittle goodies sated my cravings. It wasn't often I had spare pennies to throw away and it was a tossup in what I would choose. Standing there, mouth salivating and opting which to select, I'm sure, made Mr. Matlock a tad impatient. I'd tell him not to rush me as I hate being rushed. When St. Peter blows his horn for me I will tell him to wait a minute, just like I told Mr. Matlock. I may not get any gold stars in my crown for being so curt but by golly, don't rush me. Take a seat, read a book, run around the block but whatever you do, don't stand there tapping your feet. I may never make up my mind because I am female and it's my prerogative.

Choices were many in the line of candy. The assorted penny candy included: tootsie rolls, sugar babies, real licorice sticks (not that red yucky stuff ...

ooh, purely disgusting), candy cigarettes, Boston baked beans, root beer barrels, gum balls, salt water taffy, bit o' honey, lemon drops, tootsie pops suckers, sweet tarts, atomic fireballs, candy lips and whistles, double bubble gum, sugar daddy, milk duds, clove and beechnut gum, bazooka gum, peanut butter bars, zagnut bars, peppermint patties, slo poke suckers, cinnamon red hots and tamales and life savers. These were just a few of the great penny candies but for a child, way too many.

There were a few candies making my taste buds revolt. Anything orange or purple sent my gag reflex into action. Inside a Life Savers package, all the orange and purple candy went into file thirteen, given to the dog, buried outside or stomped to bits. It is abnormal to eat those things! I love oranges but hate orange candy. I hate grapes but love the juice and jelly. Candy of those two colors leaves a profound distaste in my mouth as the artificial flavoring is foul.

Another nasty ... I mean ... nasty, gag me to the max piece of candy is horehound. I truly believe a mad scientist, trapped inside a cubicle without benefit of oxygen and with a hatred for mankind thought of this sinister concoction. In my opinion, the tainted, vile experiment should have been left in the laboratory to blow up the idiot. Horehound was daddy's cure for a sore throat and when I asked him how it tasted, he handed me a piece. It was the first time I tried this semi conductor of puke and I spit and sputtered for a solid hour. It was as though I scarped down a wad of grapefruit rinds combined with bitter green pecans and pine tree sap. Ye Gods! There was no way to erase, wash down or brush away the flavor and my taste buds went on strike ... literally went on strike. I tried eating a mustard sandwich and couldn't taste the mustard. Daddy sat there like a bump on a log, then laughed like a wild eyed hyena at my attempt to get rid of the putrid stench and taste. The one time, bitter, gut wrenching experience would last a lifetime. The old saying is not to take candy from a stranger, but as I live and breathe, it was the last time I asked daddy for a piece of his candy.

Penny candies, as we knew the tasty morsels in the 50's, are gone, too. The slanted, glass displays or round candy jars with fingerprints etched along their perimeters or the proprietors waiting for a child to make up her mind are gone, too. While daddy is not with us anymore, I figure he is still getting a kick out of the ornery trick he played on me.

The memories...why, don't you know? In my mind, it was yesterday. The candy might have cost a penny but the memories ... priceless.

TENNIS COURT & SOFTBALL FIELD

As I opened my mail on Wednesday there was a lovely surprise from a beautiful classmate. I receive phone calls but this is the first letter from a reader regarding my Do You Remember column.

Many of you will remember Joanne Dempsey Rowe (Jody) from school as she was one of the prettiest females in Van Buren and slam dunked everyone with a vivacious personality. As a cheerleader and wearing a Kelley green skirt and white sweater with VBHS emblazoned on a green megaphone; she could turn heads quicker than you could snap your fingers. Joanne, nicknamed Jody, was homecoming maid, voted wittiest and one of the class officers. Popularity didn't deter her from being a friendly person as her smile eased anyone coming in contact with her. She knew no stranger.

Jody and her family lived on the corner of North 20th and Baldwin Streets where her mother enjoyed gardening. Walking past her house, while going to Olin Smith's Grocery Store from Izard School to grab a hamburger on lunch break, the aroma from the flower garden stopped me dead in my tracks. It was a haven of beauty with irises, daylilies, lilacs, azaleas, and a host of other tantalizing scents. At the time, I didn't know Mrs. Dempsey but she always waved, smiled, and knew in her heart, I wanted to run barefoot through her flower patch. She must have giggled knowing that I wanted to shove my face inside a giant hibiscus and picnic among the bright orange lilies. Mr. Dempsey was a tall, jovial man and could tease more than any person I ever met. Much later, in my married life when we purchased Olin Smith Grocery Store, is when I got to know both he and Mrs. Dempsey. They were young at heart and had hearts as big as the great outdoors.

Yes, Joanne, I remember so many of the things in your letter. The Teen Time Dance Party was a hoot and I was at all of the dance sessions. Brown Derby dipped cones, with a large twirl at the top; sold only at the Dairy Queen couldn't be beat. In fact, the Dairy Queen was one of my all time favorite haunts. Double features at the Bob Burns Theatre had all the teens and young kids prowling the isles. Moore's Drive-In burgers, fries and shakes were the best for miles around. There was standing room only and hardly a place to park. If you were lucky enough to have a car, it was sometimes easier to park at high school and walk the few blocks to place an order. The Press-Argus Courier has printed these stories.

The tennis court, surrounded by a high, chain link fence, was across the street from your house and it attracted tennis players in droves. It was nice to see the ladies in their short, flared, white skirts, white sweaters or blouse and white bobby socks and sneakers. It was a fashion statement. Pony tails flipped with each swing of the tennis racquet. It's a lovely picture in my mind, because now, sweats are the norm and anything goes. It's a shame the tennis court had to go by the wayside but progress sometimes gets in the way.

Progress, however, does not erase what we remember. The softball games were another part of 20th street activity with dust flying in all directions as the guys slid toward a base. All you could see were the whites of their eyes as the dirt clung to clothing, hair and skin. The area was a magnet for sports enthusiasts. The hustle and bustle went off the chart as boys and men pushed their testosterone levels to the max as they swung the bat. If you close your eyes and listen real close, the echoes can still be heard, much like the 1989 movie, Field of Dreams.

So many memories are alive and well within my vision ... through different streets I drive upon. Every blink of my eye ... in one way or the other flashes a time and place of our youth.

Regardless of how things might change in the future, or buildings / houses being razed for improvement, nothing, with the exception of a debilitating memory disease, can make us take a detour from where we were. Van Buren is alive and well with many of us who remember our old stomping grounds. Our footprints are etched on the soil and in the hallways of our respective renovated / torn down schools and hearts and initials engraved in large tree trunks can probably still be seen if you know where to look. Those reminders of a time past will not go away. Each of us, in our comprehensive, philosophical computer brain, has areas so deep with emotional attachments; the USB port is not large enough to hold all the data. We have to keep plugging them in to store more information.

The tennis court, baseball field, your wonderful parents, Olin and Pat Smith, and Olin Smith Grocery Store are effects of history. Your home place is still there. It has changed dramatically but the beauty of its grandeur is still in my psyche. Some of the things you mentioned are in stories I have written but haven't submitted. Keep reading.

Thank you, Jody, for a lovely letter and I will put it in my archives. P.S., Dan says, "Hello."

VALENTINE'S DAY

February 14 is Valentine's Day but do you know why? There is an association to martyrs and saints named Valentine as far back as medieval times. Valentine of Terni was bishop in or about AD 197. People loved him, supposedly because he was an overseer to marriage between a pagan man and a Christian woman. He was imprisoned and then beheaded by Placidus. The bones of Valentine are in a basilica in Terni, where on February 14, the town has fairs and events to commemorate Bishop Valentine.

Whether it is legend or happened, I don't know. If you ask me, it doesn't sound too romantic having your head whacked off ... so, I like my version best. It's a time when the thought of romance makes the heart flutter, the eyes can't focus, your hands shake and your legs get wobbly and spit dries up in the mouth at the sight of a possible suitor. It's an inborn trait in all of us because spring is the time for re-birth and our minds go haywire. Little girls get giddy and little boys turn shy but adults, well, they just go nuts and turn wacky as a fruitcake.

If some of you are like me, special Valentine's Day cards are squirreled away in a cedar chest or packed away among pictures. In my cedar chest is an old, hard cased album with several early nineteenth century valentines belonging to my mother. They are not like today's cards but are frilly and delicate. Some of the cards inside my cedar chest are from my grade school and others are when my children handed me their loving sentiments.

We would go to Tyler's or Sterling's, Five and Dime Stores to select cellophane covered boxes of valentine cards. Most of the verses were the same but we didn't care because it was the excitement in holding the heart palpating jewels in our hands. Taking care to print or write our names on the back of the cards, it was a chore to find the right envelope for a particular card. Not all the envelopes housed a weird shaped card and it would have to be folded, messing up the entire thing. There were bags of "Be Mine" candy hearts or larger versions of candy kisses we chose to be among the valentines to give away. Most of the time, the candy was devoured before Valentine's Day because it was a special treat.

Joyce L. Rapier

Valentine's Day in grade school was unique. The classroom ceiling was draped with red crepe paper ropes, and smocked hearts of white and red dangled in mid air. It would take my breath away as the sight of delicate, paper thin, honeycombed hearts was beautiful. About two weeks before Valentine's Day, we were allowed to decorate paper sacks with cut out hearts, crayon colored hearts of various shapes and sizes or original poems. Some of the girl's sacks had pink sheared edges decorated with lace and satin around the borders. A few were hole-punched with yarn weaving in and out the sack. Some had bright red paper roses glued atop hearts. Most of the boy's valentine sacks had their names printed on them because they didn't want any part of the frou-frou stuff. You could tell, upon sight, which gender decorated the sacks.

The week before Valentine's Day, our teacher thumb tacked the sacks to the bottom of the chalk holder beneath the blackboard and we were allowed to drop cards into sacks. Usually, it was done in secret because no one wanted to blab whom we secretly admired. If you were seen dropping a card in a sack, the school yard was buzzing with "someone's got a boyfriend or girlfriend." Then the fight and chase was on.

If Valentine's Day happened to fall midweek, we would have to wait until Friday for a last hour of school party. Parents or children were allowed to bring homemade cookies for us to enjoy while we drank cherry Kool-Aid. On occasion, we would try to sneak a peek at our cards but the teacher wouldn't allow it to happen. She would yell, "You will have the week end to look at your cards. Wait till you are home or off school ground." We were kids and anxious to see how many valentines we received. Monday was a letdown as word got around that there were those whose sacks only contained one or two. Some hearts sank, others were elated. It was a bittersweet time of youth.

NECCO candy hearts and necklaces are still available but not sold as they were in the 50's. Whimsical cellophane boxes of Valentine cards for children aren't the same. Paper Rosie and her ten cent paper roses are gone. Children's decorated paper sacks have disappeared as well as school parties and home baked cookie treats. Valentine's Day in the 50's was enthusiastic, a fabulous time for wide eyed children knowing they could surround themselves with fantasy ... even for a glorious single day.

I am glad I was able to be among those wide eyed children, because of those single days, so many years past, my heart is still young and my mind is still in harmony with Valentine's Day.

Joyce L. Rapier

STILTS

One of the homemade toys tickling our fancy was homemade stilts. Those contraptions didn't tickle anything but managed to skin knees, make you stump your toes and crack you in the chin if it caught you off guard. Did it keep us from climbing on the small rail? No. It was like a magnet stuck to stupid!

If a kid was lucky enough to find two planks without splinters, at least one foot taller than the person climbing aboard, had nails and a hammer and could keep from thwacking the thumb, then he was almost in business. Next, you had to find two smaller pieces of wood at least the width of the plank and somewhere secret to hammer the sections together. Most often, a father could be heard yelling, "Get out of my tools and don't be wasting the nails. I never know when something will fall apart."

Careful to make sure no one was watching, bam, bam, bam went the hammer. A few foul words would color the air from overzealous boys trying in vain to maneuver a loose brain. I began to think their thumbs resembled hammer head sharks from all the bent nails lying on the ground. Sometimes a knot in the plank would be hit and shatter portions of the wood or weaken the whole shebang. When it happened, they would drag home another plank ... where they got it is another story. I didn't ask and they didn't tell but someone must have missed some of their inventory. Sometimes there was a pile of split wood two feet high. Not to worry though, it would be used for a precarious tree house.

Anyway, after a confab between the boys as to who would get the honors of holding the nail, the construction of stilts would resume. Placing the long piece of wood on the ground, the smaller sections would be nailed about one foot from the base. It had to have a brace under it so the boys would sneak a handsaw and cut triangular pieces for support. Before long, the stilts, resembling an over sized tomato stake, were made and I must say they did a good job.

The hard task of climbing on to the stilts left a lot to be desired. Holding one stilt in one hand and balancing the other at an angle, a foot was placed on the narrow wood rail. Remember, the rail is one foot from the bottom, one leg is up in the air and the other foot is trying to maintain control of a wayward, second stilt. It was not uncommon to back onto a hard surface or hold on to another person's head while trying to mount the stilts. It was a slapstick comedy of errors. After a few pump knots on the forehead and splinters the size of toothpicks stuck in a rear end, leg or hand, the boys began to walk. Thunk, thunk, thunk was the sound of stilts hitting rocks in the road, but their prowess, in achieving power to manhandle wood, was their "strut."

I tried the silly one foot stilts ... one time, and decided if they wanted to crack a skull, bruise a part of their anatomy for macho sake or eat the wood for breakfast ... go for it. It made me do the splits in the air and almost cloned me from a natural state.

You would think having armpits crammed full of wood, in the fashion of large crutches without padding, would deter them from wanting to scale tall buildings. It didn't. You would also think having teeth mash into the lips or black rings around the eyes like a raccoon would stop them dead in their tracks. Not so. They thrived and fed on antics doing bodily harm. Having the body one foot from the ground was a piece of cake but they weren't satisfied. Why not two feet off the ground, two feet up in the air?

Into the wood pile went the one foot stilts and out came the two foot omen of kismet ... attached by old, wire bedspring coils. Now, why they needed to be so high in the air, on two blister making, bonk, boing, bonk, apparatuses just to prove a point, was beyond me. Bouncing up in the air on two pieces of wood and having air whistle air between the legs, was not my cup of tea. Far be it from me to stop them but I did enjoy seeing the "tomato stakes," hair, and bed springs go flying into the wild blue yonder while their derrières hit the ground. A few sessions of pillow sitting or ice packs to soothe the wounded rump grounded them for awhile but back on the stilts they went. They were impervious to pain and sometimes thought they were invincible. What is in the male gender that makes them push themselves into oblivion, just to prove a point or say, "I did it my way?"

The days of the stilts were comical and a way to appease a lazy summer vacation. It was just a part of youth's growth and fun times of the 50's. If a picture, of bygone days, is worth a thousand words, then my memory picture of the boys on bedspring stilts is beyond thousands of words ... it's hung in infinity and priceless.

PEANUTS AND COKE BOTTLES

Listening to the radio, Barbara Mandrell and George Jones were singing, "I Was Country, When Country Wasn't Cool." A line from a verse, "I was putting peanuts in my coke," reminded me why I liked the bottle but not the cola. Not to mention, it ruined peanuts by drowning them in a sea of caramel colored, hiccup inducing, effervescent kidney shakers and bladder swells. I called the concoction "movers and shakers." Not that it affected world news or made someone a renowned Rhodes Scholar but because it shook my innards like a raging volcano. Peanuts and coke do not mix and neither do vinegar and soda.

Coke used to be in a 6.5 ounce, traditional contoured bottle where they were stored in a large, open top ice box in a grocery store. Lift the lid and bottles of Coke, Grapette and Orange sodas were deeply embedded in mounds of ice. Sometimes the ice melted making the water so cold it would numb the hands. Daddy loved Coca-Cola and Grapette. I couldn't stomach either one of them. One because it was purple and the other was too blasted fizzy. Having a few empty cola bottles did come in handy and so did the bag of peanuts my grandma had in her kitchen.

When I was in junior high at J.J. Izard, a science fair was held. Those students, wanting to contribute something to be judged, set out in their endeavors to claim the coveted first, second, third and honorable mention ribbons. My best friend and I decided to try our skill in building one of the science projects. Unfortunately, my mother and dad were in an automobile accident and my sister and I were staying at my Grandma Hawkins' house on Knox Street. My friend and I couldn't get together to do the project, so I opted to do it by myself and add her name to the entry. Since the car was totaled, mother was in the hospital and daddy was afoot, I was in a quandary. What on earth would I do for the project and how would I get it to school? Ingenuity, two hands to juggle it and two walking feet.

Grandma had a box of Plaster of Paris, a roll of gauze, a six-pack of empty Coke bottles, a sack of raw peanuts and a little bit of old, crumbling, red rouge she bought at Tyler's Five and Dime Store. All I needed was water and a pile of small rocks. Placing three bottles together, tied with a bit of twine, my project began to take form. I dipped each piece of gauze into the water and plaster, forming it around the bottles in cone fashion. It took a while for successive wraps to dry, but before long the massive volcano took shape. When it was about completed, the rocks were hinged in place to resemble lava. It was a masterpiece but heavy as lead.

Grandma laughed and said, "What will you do to make it explode?" Remembering a little trick mother used, I gathered the necessary ingredients. I poured a half cup of baking soda into each of the 6.5 ounce bottles and added the red rouge. Thinking it wasn't enough to look real; I added a few peanuts to top off the mixture. The last ingredient would wait. It was the pièce de résistance. Somebody, namely judges, would be in for the shock of their life. What would happen to me and my friend was anybody's guess!

I am not sure how I got the thing to school. It was cumbersome and lopsided. Walking down the boulder laden hill on Knox Street, the volcano was eager to jump out of my hands to beat me to the bottom of the hill. My arms were heavy from lugging my books and balancing the volcano but I managed, by divine intervention, to get to school. It was a relief to place the idiot thing on one of the cafeteria tables where judging would begin after the bell rang. Near the volcano, I placed a small container full of liquid with instructions to the judges to pour it into each of the volcano openings. I knew what would happen and wished I could be there to see the expressions on their faces. Take my word for it, I heard about it later.

After the judging was complete, someone told me "we" won a blue ribbon for second place and a yellow ribbon for ingenuity but to be careful when we retrieved them. Some of the judges were a tad irate! When I went to the cafeteria, the volcano and ribbons were gone and the table my volcano sat upon was a mess. White powder, red rouge and crushed peanuts were scattered all over the place. My small container of liquid was void. It appeared, when the judges began pouring my secret ingredient ... vinegar ... into the three coke bottles, the baking soda and vinegar bubbled, spewing rouge, smelly vinegar and soda and peanuts into the air and on their clothing. They thought it was ingenious but not "cool."

Lucky for me, my friend tossed the volcano in the trash and I didn't have to tote it home. She kept the ribbons. No, I didn't like drinking colas or thinking peanuts in cokes was "cool" or was upset about not taking home a ribbon. In my mind, I won a red ribbon because shoving peanuts inside the Molotov, vinegar and soda cocktail, proved one thing. I might have lived in the city but "I Was Country, When Country Wasn't Cool."

Joyce L. Rapier

VICTORY GARDENS

When I was a little girl we had a vegetable garden stretching the length of the lower portion of our backyard butting up to a wire fence. Corn grew as high as the arms could reach and yielded the sweetest tender morsels. I loved to jerk the husks off and eat it before it was cooked. Okra, the sharp spindle darts, was next to the corn and it made me itch. Then there were green beans and sweet peas twining around wire stretched between tall poles. Lower growing plants were eggplant, cucumbers, yellow bumpy squash, cabbage, luscious tomatoes, onions and lettuce. Come winter the cold crops took their spots. We had enough food for Cox's army and shared with family and friends. Mother canned food and it's why I still can food today. Every year I go to Larry and Sharon Black's tomato farm and purchase tomatoes to make many quarts of hot salsa, spaghetti, pizza and BBQ sauces, tomato juice and my version of V8 juice and other condiments for winter foods. It tastes better being homemade and I love to can. I freeze what I can't can and it tides us over for the winter.

Almost everyone I knew had a garden even if it was only a small area in their yard. It was a necessity just as it is becoming a necessity for a lot of people in the year 2008. With food prices skyrocketing from the demands of transportation fuel, those price increases trickle down to the consumer. One way or the other all of us will see the need for making a victory garden.

Victory gardens, also called war gardens, were planted because of World Wars I and II. People in the USA were planting vegetables, herbs and fruit gardens because it would reduce tremendous pressure on public foods. It was also lowering the price for the US War Department to help feed the troops and at the same time allowing them to spend money for military defense. This was an effort on our part to do what we, as a nation, had to do while the wars continued. It was a morale booster for the citizens to know they could contribute to the labor force and be fulfilled by feeding their own families. People used any area available to them to plant gardens whether it was on a roof top or lawn. Various sections of state property were plowed under to make Victory gardens.

When WWII ceased, a lot of citizens stopped planting because of the expectation of greater things to come, and slowly, the Victory gardens disappeared and flowers were planted to celebrate a new beginning. The only remaining "vegetable" Victory garden "holdovers" were from those persons remembering what it was like to be rationed of food supplies. It was not just comestibles but rationing of sugar, flour and basic necessities to survive.

It's hard to believe the year 2008 could digress in the direction of Victory gardens but more and more families are plowing up land to plant those Victory gardens to survive the ever rising food prices. With gasoline prices draining the pocketbooks, it will take a toll on everyone to provide for their families. It seems, the more we advance to further our ability to be the richest country in the world, the more we slide backward. It wouldn't be such a bad thing to have a garden as it would be our "morale booster" to thwart off the need to be so dependent on the importers. Sure, we would have to purchase the condiments, flour and sugar but it would cut down the cost of buying many vegetables. If we had access to local egg farmers and fruit suppliers to support their way of life, we would be better off in the long haul. If any of you are out there, give me a call!

You're thinking... what about the time and electricity/gas it takes to can all these vegetables? Where would I store them? How much is this going to cost? I don't know how to can. I don't have the time to devote or the resources to do these things. Electricity/gas costs are soaring. There are only two of us and it is cheaper to buy in small quantities. I am too old to dig in the dirt and what if I don't have enough land to plant more than one tomato plant? It's hard work and it gets too hot in the summer.

This is where the local vegetable markets come into play. Many of the vendors have great products and they need the money more than the giant retailers as they do this service to the community to survive and to support a family. For those persons who love to garden, don't mind sweating as you toil for the fruits of your labor, a lot of the vegetables you grow could be shared with the less fortunate. There is another service called "bartering." I know this may sound ridiculous but if the citizens of the USA could band together while WWI & II were in full force, we can now. Oh, well, it's just a thought... maybe a pipedream!

As for my family, I will continue to grow vegetables in my small Victory garden, plow up the backyard if necessary, and in the meantime, support the local vegetable markets.

GEM STONES AND BUTTER

Where would we be without memories? Everywhere we go and everything we do can trigger a moment in time. Some memories are precious gem stones made of diamonds, rubies, sapphires and emeralds, but sometimes they might appear as crumbling rocks. Our gems are manmade, not those from million years in the making, but coated, in a sense, with mounds of laughter, pain, traumatic earth shattering events and lauds of praise. Photographs, stuffed inside a shoe box, hung on a wall or in an album or scattered in a dresser drawer, are time frozen in an instant. Most of them can make you remember the time and place, why it was taken, what you were wearing and if it was fun or sad. A scent is powerful as it pulls not only the picture but surroundings and makes it come alive. Visual effects can make a person search for lost or mislaid items and to touch an inanimate object jolts you into remembering why you received it or who gave it to you. What someone says can activate the essence of time, because all of us whether we know one another, have experienced similar happenings. Every one of these actions or senses is gem stones, created only by us to be remembered by us. A gentle nudge is all it takes to drift toward a nostalgic moment.

The reason I ask where we would be without memories is because two lovely ladies phoned me. One lady told me my story about lye soap made fond "gem stones" within her cherished circle of recollections, spread ten-fold. Another sweet lady said her "gem stone" was salt pork bacon, but unlike my combination with biscuits, hers was cornbread. Her husband wrote for the Press-Argus Courier before his passing in November of 2008. Even though our paths haven't physically crossed, the conversations we shared were equivalent to events. We spoke about the Schaible dairy farm located on Oliver Springs Road now called Pointer Trail. It was a dirt road. The old home place, as you might remember, was recently razed. It sat directly in front of Coleman Junior High School. The two story house, built around 1910, was large for its size but small in comparison to houses of today. It had exterior walls at least twelve inches thick. At one time the grounds were meticulously groomed with Magnolia trees spanning the front yard. It was picture perfect.

The Schaible's moved from Oregon to Van Buren in 1900. How do I know? Bess Schaible Rapier was my husband's grandmother. The property of Matt Schaible, Bess's father, spanned across I-40 and atop the hill where the new houses sit and to the east adjacent to Skinny Stamps' property. All of it was vast pasture land. After Matt's death, the property was owned by Roy Schaible, Matt's son. Across the road and to the south east of the home place was a dairy farm, owned by Jim Schaible, Roy's brother. It was where North Park Baptist Church is now located. A tad further east was where Bess's sister, Anna (Aunt Annie) Schaible McKnight and her husband, Sam, lived. David Cathey, step-son to Jim Schaible, wrote many articles about the Schaible's dairy farm. Due to deaths and progress, these lovely gem stones are memories.

Our nickname for Bess was "Ma Virie." She was a wealth of information when she was not in the garden hoeing weeds or puttering around in her flower garden. Her activities kept her young at heart and several of them are indelible in her teachings to me. Each day was set aside for household chores, doing handcrafts (she taught me how to do drawn work) or baking. Saturday, we always went to visit Ma Virie and Pa Val Rapier. She was usually baking homemade rolls and resisting them was not in our vocabulary.

On the table sat a small chunk of homemade butter, unusually delicious and tempting. Asking her if she used a butter churn as she did when she was a child, she just laughed. "Not any more. I do it the easy way." She passed along to me, the secret of her butter and how to make it. It became a delightful thing to do, especially on Thanksgiving or when my children needed something to while away their boredom. It always worked and they felt a sense of pride knowing they contributed to an evening meal. Now, I am passing it along to all of you so your children can have a small memory to file away in their own treasures.

You will need a glass quart jar with a tight lid. Don't use plastic jars. I use a mason canning jar but you could use any clean, empty jar as long as it has a tight lid. Pour one pint of heavy whipping cream into the jar. Do not add salt! Gently shake it (takes a little while) until it forms small slivers of butter on the sides of the jar. You will begin to see the whey separate from the cream and butter will adhere to the glass container. Soon a ball of butter will form in a small chunk on the bottom of the glass jar. When the whey is more than the ball of butter, pour off the whey but continue to shake, just for a minute or two because it needs to stay in ball form. Drop the ball of butter on to a plate and wipe away any excess whey. Now you can add a touch of salt, chives, garlic powder or other spice. Refrigerate and enjoy.

Like I said, where would we be without special "gem stones" and those who taught us?

STRING PICTURES & YO-YO'S

As I approached the checkout at CV's on Pointer Trail, Jane Moses, a delightful checker with a sunny disposition, was doodling with a circle of string. She was trying to remember how to make a cup and saucer and almost had it mastered. I told her I could do it. Well, my cup and saucer turned upside down and my second try was not what I expected. Part of the string I should have looped, looped in the opposite direction making a handle on the cup. Before I left CV's, I told her a piece of string would be attached to my hip until I remembered how to do it as well as Jacob's Ladder and other fun string pastimes. When I got home and put away my groceries, I grabbed up a piece of green yarn tucked away in my sewing kit and began making the cup and saucer. I hadn't forgotten and it unfolded right before my eyes.

It was a fun thing to do when I was a kid because there weren't too many activities to keep the brain in "go" mode. Sure, we had comic books but after awhile, we would sit around and twiddle our thumbs from boredom. My curiosity got the better of me and I did a quick search on the internet to find out where and how string pictures made their debut in the world. It's anyone's guess but it appears it has been around for many centuries. According to my web source, many cultures may have used the string designs in rituals or other areas of importance. Who is to know? Not me. It also states sitting around campfires, someone might use the string puppets or designs as illustrations. The web site gives all kinds of directions in making a cup and saucer, Eiffel tower, Jacob's Ladder, Hand Catch, and believe it or not, how to make your own string and create water in the desert.

Remembering how to make these pictures with string brought to mind the "crack me in the teeth" toy. What is a quiz, Prince of Wales Toy, bandalore, l'emigrette and incroyable? They are words used for the common yo-yo by the British and French. Yo-yo means "come back" and was used in the Philippines as a weapon. Those particular large yo-yos were attached to twenty foot ropes and had studs and sharp barbs. The first time any American heard the term yo-yo was in 1920 when Pedro Flores, an emigrant from the Philippines, produced them in California. People might think D.F. Duncan was the inventor. He wasn't but bought the rights from Flores and then trademarked

Duncan Yo-Yo. It is the second oldest toy, (doll is first), in the world and garnered the honors of being the first toy in outer space. Donald Duncan's empire folded in 1962 due to overzealous production (sold 45 million units) and advertising. Even with abundant sales, costs exceeded net worth. Sound familiar?

The first Duncan Yo-Yo I had was bright yellow. Slipping the loop over my finger was easy but making it roll back up the string took a bit of doing. Mother kept telling me I wasn't holding my mouth right. Apparently keeping the mouth slightly ajar or biting the edge of the tongue was the trick when dangling the round piece of wood to the floor. It was a trick all right, when she told me to jerk and let it roll up the stupid string. It plastered me in the mouth knocking out a baby tooth, then fell to the floor and ricocheted straight to my right eye and forehead. I had the biggest shiner in history and a pump knot to boot.

Getting it to do the sleeper, walk the dog or whirl it in the air was not one of my finest talents because it was bound and determined to waylay the dickens out of me. I believe, although it didn't have a twenty foot rope or barbs attached to it, my yo-yo came out of the ice age, hell bent for leather to do me bodily harm. After my finger turned black from too tight a string, I had a wild fight with the cockeyed thing as I tried to disassemble it from my finger. It went inside a drawer and didn't, ever again, see light of day. It was not a toy I became attached to or fond of because of its insidious behavior.

All the kids in my neighborhood (sans me) were adept with the yo-yo. Making string pictures was a snap and kept kid's minds and hands out of the devil's workshop. I feel blessed because the fortune bell rang for me today, not with money or any lucky streak, but by mere accident. If I hadn't been in CV's grocery store, Jane and her kind act of hand maneuvering with string might have laid dormant on my list of memories. Now, the dexterity of hand and string can resume while striking a chord of the simple, lazy, hazy days of time trapped in the past. The green loop of yarn, snipped from its snug resting place, is alive and lying on my office desk. It will be picked up on occasion to remind me the simple, unencumbered things in life are free.

http://www.wikihow.com/Make-the-Cup-and-Saucer-With-String

OLD SAYINGS & PHRASES

The other day a gentleman named Carl phoned me and asked if I lived in the past. This was my reply. "The future is nothing but the past, relived. What has been will be because traditions or things are passed from generation to generation and it is how we learn. You can't live in the future without having lived in the past because lives are cyclic." There was dead silence on the phone when I asked if he was still connected. A big laugh generated from the end of the line when he said, "My, how time flies. I didn't think of it that way."

I asked his last name and he said, "Ask me no questions, I'll tell you no lies." We talked for at least an hour and by the time we finished our conversation, I was laughing so hard, tears streamed down my cheeks. He was a puff of fresh air and our hour long play on words was refreshing.

Later, one of the phrases he used rambled around in my brain. I thought of many old sayings and phrases I have heard from my grandparents and relatives. So, grab a pencil and paper or peck the keyboard and join me for some fun. Give it a lick and a promise. Let's just sit around and chew the fat. It'll be child's play. Does it give you a clue?

My, how time flies but our conversation didn't fly, it floated like a bird on the wind. With his sage advice, he's a diamond in the rough, I thought. He wasn't a fish out of the water, or paddling a canoe upstream, but a man with a heart as big as Texas. He was a legend in his own time and knew a little knowledge is a dangerous thing, but wasn't a man of few words. I wondered if he had an ace up his sleeve and how it would be played. Little did he know I would take the ace and run with it and write this story. I heard what he said and it was clear as a bell and was bright as a new silver dollar.

"I'll give you a penny for your thoughts," he said. "A poor man's memories could be a rich man's goal as a rolling stone gathers no moss. A wise man listens to his conscience knowing there is a time for all seasons, and a man's word is as good as his bond." I ascertained this gentleman was as honest as the day is long, and like me, could spin a tale as long as a country mile, or at least as the crow flies.

How we managed to talk about dogs is beyond me but it brought to mind these one-liners. Back in the good old days, the back seat driver had a bird's eye view. If you got out of a car, you'd think barking dogs seldom bite. Why, they are just barking in the wind. Perhaps they are barking up the wrong tree. Nope, some dogs are bad to the bone, and don't beat around the bush when it comes to taking a chunk out of the bone. You will run like the dickens or bend like a willow or break like an oak! Sometimes you're between a rock and a hard place, or betwixt and between, and hope the dog is wearing blinders. You will hope you don't break a leg when this bright eyed and bushy tailed critter decides to bring home the bacon looking for brownie points from its master. Its confrontation is like the calm before the storm because every dog has his day.

For crying out loud, do you think I am giving you a cock and bull story? Far be it from me! To coin a phrase, you might think this story is corny as a cup of corn and I am crazy as a Bessie bug but it's all cut and dried. I am sober as a judge. Don't count your chickens before they hatch and don't take any wooden nickels because fact is stranger than fiction. Things are seldom far and few between and for what it's worth I'm not four aces short of a deck. I'm not pulling your leg and I do not go off half cocked. Hang loose and we will get there together.

Hold your horses! I double dog dare you to play hide and seek with your mind. I can feel it in my bones you won't let this go in one ear and out the other.

It's a piece of cake as you just had a brain storm to keep the ball rolling as out of the mouths of babes come all wise sayings. It's mind over matter. If you don't mind, it doesn't matter.

Let's give each other a pat on the back because pearls of wisdom will make us proud as a peacock as we rack the brain to do rank and file. Root hog or die and strike while the iron is hot because the best things in life are free.

The game is afoot so write while you may. Put down on paper sayings come your way. The long and short of it is the more things change the more they stay the same. The night is far gone, the day is at hand, and the sky is the limit. Don't sit around and say you can't do it as time's a wasting.

I hope you've enjoyed these old time sayings and phrases and written down the ones you remember. Hold your mouth right and give it a try and find my 101 phrases. Mark my words, there are thousands to write. At this point in time, I've wrapped it up and that's it in a nutshell.

Answers:

1. The future is nothing but the past
2. What has been will be

3. Dead silence
4. My, how time flies
5. Ask me no questions, I'll tell you no lies
6. A puff of fresh air
7. Play on words
8. Rambled around in my brain
9. Give it a lick and a promise
10. Sit around and chew the fat
11. It'll be child's play
12. Bird on the wind
13. A diamond in the rough
14. A fish out of the water
15. Paddling a canoe upstream
16. A heart as big as Texas
17. A legend in his own time
18. A little knowledge is a dangerous thing
19. A man of few words
20. An ace up his sleeve
21. Run with it
22. Clear as a bell
23. Bright as a new silver dollar
24. A penny for your thoughts
25. A poor man's memories could be a rich man's goal
26. A rolling stone gathers no moss
27. A wise man listens to his conscience
28. A time for all seasons

29. A man's word is as good as his bond
30. As honest as the day is long
31. As long as a country mile
32. As the crow flies
33. Back in the good old days
34. Back seat driver
35. Bird's eye view
36. Barking dogs seldom bite
37. Barking in the wind
38. Barking up the wrong tree
39. Bad to the bone
40. Don't beat around the bush
41. Taking a chunk out of the bone
42. Run like the dickens
43. Bend like a willow or break like an oak
44. You're between a rock and a hard place
45. Betwixt and between
46. Wearing blinders
47. Break a leg
48. Bright eyed and bushy tailed
49. Bring home the bacon
50. Brownie points
51. Calm before the storm
52. Every dog has his day
53. For crying out loud
54. Cock and bull story

55. Far be it from me
56. Coin a phrase
57. Corny as a cup of corn
58. Crazy as a Bessie bug
59. All cut and dried
60. Sober as a judge
61. Don't count your chickens before they hatch
62. Don't take any wooden nickels
63. Fact is stranger than fiction
64. Seldom far and few between
65. For what it's worth
66. Four aces short of a deck
67. Pulling your leg
68. Go off half cocked
69. Hang loose
70. Hold your horses
71. I double dog dare you
72. Hide and seek
73. I can feel it in my bones
74. In one ear and out the other
75. It's a piece of cake
76. Just had a brain storm
77. Keep the ball rolling
78. Out of the mouths of babes come all wise sayings
79. Mind over matter
80. If you don't mind, it doesn't matter

81. A pat on the back
82. Pearls of wisdom
83. Proud as a peacock
84. Rack the brain
85. Rank and file
86. Root hog or die
87. Strike while the iron is hot
88. The best things in life are free
89. The game is afoot
90. Sayings come your way
91. The long and short of it
92. The more things change the more they stay the same
93. The night is far gone, the day is at hand
94. The sky is the limit
95. You can't do it
96. Time's a wasting
97. Hold your mouth right
98. Give it a try
99. Mark my words
100. At this point in time
101. I've wrapped it up
102. That's it in a nutshell

TRUANT OFFICERS

While standing in a checkout line at a store, I was talking with two of my friends about kids running amok. Our conversation was nothing out of the ordinary as the topic affects parents and children of the twenty-first century, but is it relative to other centuries? The Classical Greek Philosopher, Socrates, of 469 BC said, "The children now love luxury; they have bad manners, contempt for authority; they show disrespect for elders and love chatter in place of exercise. Children are now tyrants, not the servants of their households. They no longer rise when elders enter the room. They contradict their parents, chatter before company, gobble up dainties at the table, cross their legs, and tyrannize their teachers."

When I was going to school, you can bet your sweet little Petunia; the kids did not run rampant, contradict their parents or tyrannize the teachers. Kids were not in control of the household, sass or talk back to the parents or have contempt of authority. They did not demand more than the parents could provide. On occasion, you might hear of a wayward kid but it was rare. Know why? Parents, teachers, and law enforcement Russell, Wilbanks, Black and other officers had control.

Back then, the town was small and everyone knew one another. If a kid decided to skip school, he / she couldn't hide because within twenty minutes someone saw "little Johnny or Mary" and phoned the parents. No one hesitated to say, "I saw your kid walking the tracks or he / she was looking in the window of Langston's Drug Store." Kids at school knew when someone was in deep trouble because they couldn't "sit" down the next day.

Teachers were allowed corporal punishment (I don't mean beatings ... I mean a swat with the board of education). I do not condone any type of mental or physical abuse, but in my opinion, there is a difference between physical torture and a swat across the derrière. The only time a kid suffered pain was when their "dignity" was embarrassed. Most times it took only one swat to straighten out a supercilious kid. After an episode with the principal, the parents performed the parental "board of education" at home. It didn't kill any of us to be straightened out from a life of crime. You might say we had more respect for those persons who kept us in line. However, some kids think they know it all and just will not listen!

One person, making a determined impression on all the kids, was the truant officer. He didn't take any flack from anyone and did his job corralling a "wannabe" truant kid. Kids didn't have too many cars and their feet were their mode of transportation. Trust the truant officer to know every nook and cranny where those feet would tread. He was a wily character and would crawl inside drainage cans to pull out a kid, place them in a police car and take them back to school. Most kids, when they heard the term "truant officer," cringed because this authority figure laid down the law. Many times we could hear, "Just take me to jail but don't call my dad."

We would do a proverbial sigh because we knew why they didn't want dad to find out they had been caught with a hand in the cookie jar. Dads were the figurehead of a household and wouldn't put up with nonsense, especially when respect was at stake. The parents held the reign and kept the children in check. They were not friends but parents ... parents, whose only aim in life, was to love and provide for their children and maintain control until they came of age. When the kids moved out, they didn't sponge off their parents, as so many do today. Truant officer ... by definition didn't mean ... "I can get away with anything."

Today, it's not the norm. Teachers are not allowed to do any type of punishment for fear of being sued or losing their license to teach. We have police at schools, shutdowns when news reports contain horrors of school terrorizing, and courtrooms full of kids out of control. Parents are afraid to punish a child because the kids are in control of them and lash out if they are told "no." Kids scream when they can't have something at a store and scream some more until a parent gives in to their whim. It seems to be a vicious cycle, a cycle of kids in control ... not parents.

There is no such thing as a generation gap but it is a wide communication gap. It is merely an age difference with a test of wills and enabling ... key word ... enabling. These same symptoms, we experience today, were noticed and at an all time high in 469 BC. Kids are human, experience human frailties, have fears, and want to be accepted by their peers, regardless of the outcome ... good or bad. When parents and kids figure out what Walt Kelly's, *Pogo,* meant when he said, "I have met the enemy and he is Me." everyone will figure out the problem.

If kids and parents survived the "test of wills" in Socrates time ... surely to goodness parents can just say no and add if you are stupid enough to do the crime ... you will do the time!

ST. PATRICK'S DAY

Aye, me darlin', tis St. Paddy's Day, th' time fer feastin' un a'wearin'o' th' green. Maybe tis legend fer th' shamrock ta be holdin' ta th' Trinity but tis a mighty thought knowin' th' three petals be harborin' th' love of th' Irish fer th' Holy week. Believin' th' green, tis all can be seen, brings March like th' mighty, aye, love, cometh spring.

St. Patrick's Day is right up there with the man in the moon, leprechauns hiding to snatch up what you have in your pocket, and the gold at the end of the rainbow. Everyone who enjoys the lively pipe and fiddle music, singing Danny Boy or When Irish Eyes Are Smiling, brogue of tongue, imbibing a wee too much of whiskey or believing they are Irish, can relate to one another.

Everyone in grade school loved the week of St. Patrick's Day. Shamrocks decorated hallways, classrooms and lapels of teachers and students. Scared to not wear green, kids plastered themselves with bits of green to keep from getting pinched. Some, in their desire to inflict fingernail gouges, would bruise the arms or leave blood blisters on unsuspecting prey.

Black and blue marks covered arms and most often, the rear end. When the teacher asked if any of us were Irish, hands flew into the air.

I am not sure if it was the romantic thought of being Irish or if our imaginations ran rampant on ideas of tiny leprechauns and gnomes hiding in bushes. It's magical for a child to envision grandiose pictures of tiny fairies and wee people living under giant toadstools and searching for the illusive pot of gold when they see a rainbow. Maybe it is the luck of the Irish to be able to spin a tale of pointed toed sprites as they sneak from their hiding places to scatter fairy dust. Whatever it is, the Emerald Isle is alive and well with folk lore, green top hats, meerschaum pipes puffing smoke rings in the air and banshees.

I was one of those students raising the hand, proud to be of Irish ancestry. Quite frankly, I didn't have a clue if I was Irish but it was exciting to think so. Part Cherokee, yes, but I wouldn't find out about other blood lines until I was grown. Searching for ancestry, I came across written notes that were among those from my aunt, Margaret Brannam Harmon, my father's sister. It's a very long story from generation to generation and I won't elaborate but to say, my great-grandfather, Christopher Columbus Brannam, was the father to Clero Evelyn Brannam who married Lucien

Bacon Huckelbury in March 1897. It's how I came to have the information. Reading all the notes, I found out my heritage wasn't too far off the spectrum. On my father's side, even though the notes did not actually say for certain, I think I may be part Scottish.   However, a strange occurrence made me find out another piece of my heritage. My maternal grandmother, Evaline Hawkins, was hospitalized with a brown recluse spider bite. My sister, Hazel and I were sitting in her hospital room having a normal conversation. Grandma, having been sedated and under the influence of powerful drugs, began talking in Irish brogue. Our mouths gaped at hearing grandma rattle a full blown conversation ... a conversation neither one of us understood. Disbelief and in unison to one another we said, "Did you hear that? She's talking in a heavy Irish dialect."

We couldn't wait for grandma to come out from under anesthetics to find out to whom she was talking to and what she was saying. The next day when grandma was lucid, we repeated part of what she said. She smiled and told us she was talking to her deceased father, John Henry Jones, an Irish immigrant who married Sarah Belle Honey, a Cherokee. Up to this point, being Irish was only speculation. Now, it was fact.

Like all little kids at school, I pretended being Irish. I enjoyed paper cut shamrocks, finding a lucky four leaf clover, doing the Irish clog and jigs and wondering, at times, why I could twirl the tongue with an Irish flavor. I don't have to wonder or pretend anymore. I am part Irish.

By the time you read this, St. Patrick's Day will have drifted into the sunset. The shamrocks will be put away and the green will disappear. We will have to wait another year to celebrate the lively festivities, pinching and hunting the pot of gold. So, this part Irish Lass wishes all of you a happy belated St. Patrick's Day. May you always have walls for the winds, a roof for the rain, tea beside the fire, laughter to cheer you, those you love near you, and all your heart might desire!

STONEHENGE & FLINTSTONE MOUNTAIN

The earth has strange mysteries. People wonder how the majestic Stonehenge came to be and why it was structured. Standing 330 feet in diameter, it must be one of the most phenomenal sites on planet earth. Was it a monument to earthlings, an altar for sacrifice or prayer, or a calendar to predict astronomical events? Speculations have been around for centuries but none of us will ever know for certain what went through the minds of those who built it. How did they know how to place the stones in proper alignment for the sun in conjunction with the moon's orbit? Another thing puzzling the minds of scientists is how anyone with mortal strength could move the colossal stones? Was it an army of desperate men and women whose design was to baffle those who would question its structure? Clearly, with all the supposition, no one will fully understand or comprehend the magnitude for which it was intended. Perhaps we aren't meant to question its author, age or power, but to marvel in its grandeur.

On our green "Flintstone" acre of property stands a small deliberately placed Stonehenge. When we built our house, the land was full of rocks. Some were small and some, well ... they were probably here when Stonehenge was erected. Needless to say, Mount Vista, a.k.a., Flintstone Mountain had to be part of the growing change during the Ice Age, when the earth's crust rocked and rolled from horrendous volcanic eruptions. Some rocks are maneuverable but other rocks stand firm as powerful subjects beneath the feet.

When we decided to construct a vegetable garden behind our house, we laid out the width and depth. It couldn't take up all the land because our children needed a place to play ... when they weren't working in the garden. Yes, they worked in the garden and even thought we were miserable parents making them do a chore they found intolerable. The most contemptible job of their tenure in the garden was to move rocks ... those massive, immovable Stonehenge rocks. They mumbled under their breath "we are part of the Flintstone clan" when a rock was removed because other large rocks stirred upward. It was as though the earth was rising up under their feet to shatter the desire for play.

I do believe there is a power higher than mortal man who wants to keep children in check.

Otherwise, we would not have had tired little kids falling asleep when the lights went out at night. Were my kid's saints? No, because they dubbed us Wilma and Fred. No child alive is a saint and my children didn't wear halos ... unless you can call the sweat beads forming around their foreheads, halos. Even wearing homemade angel wings for a Christmas pageant didn't keep them from wanting to become a minion of the devil. As they grew in their penchant for rebellion, our form of punishment, when they became unruly, was the chain gang ... aptly called in our household ... rock crushing. They despised those rocks even though we told them hard work would build character. All the rocks around my flowerbeds are gratuitous formations from my two sons and the miniature Stonehenge that was secreted beneath the earth.

As we were down on bony knees praying for Divine intervention, we can give thanks to God the kids are grown, viable and taxpaying citizens. They are not banging rocks while wearing ankle bracelets. They have vegetable gardens and rock bordered flowerbeds.

One rock, still standing from the sledge hamming duo, has been all over our yard. In 1973, it started out in the garden as a boulder the size of a pick-up truck. With the help of a chain and Dan's pick-up, it moved inside a flower bed. It didn't look right, so it was moved to another location. Out of order in its natural state, it was used as a bench. Still not right so it was moved to the vacant lot next door. Shoot, we had to bring it back when neighbors began building their house. It was a danged eyesore. What to do with this blasted rock? It couldn't be broken or used as an ornament around the neck, but it was, figuratively speaking, a millstone. Our last resort was to stand it upright and with the aid of a friend and his backhoe, we did. It was finally a piece of beauty where we could enjoy seeing our boys' handiwork. It needed something but what?

Last winter, 2008, the rock was tilting and we were afraid one of our grandchildren would be hurt if it fell. Trying to push it back where it stood, it did fall ... with a thud! It stayed on the ground because Dan and I couldn't man handle the thousand pound rock. The rock was where it wanted to be and we resigned ourselves to leave it alone. On Saturday, the day before Easter and Christ's resurrection, the duo rock crushers came to our rescue. It was, after all, their rock ... a rock more powerful than the two of them who kept them on a solid foundation. Using two pry bars and their strength, the boys and our daughter-in-law lifted it and wedged it securely inside a deep trench.

The world does have strange mysteries but our Stonehenge is not a mystery. It's a miracle of two boys and their success. As I hugged their necks, they smiled knowing they rescued their childhood nemesis. Once again our Stonehenge was resurrected, upright in its glory and the brass plate fastened to its front was clearly visible ... Grannie and Paw Paw's Stonehenge, 1973.

ASAFOETIDA
(Asafetida)

Some of you won't know what asafetida is and be thankful for it. I guarantee you one thing, if you ever smelled it, you wouldn't forget the stench. For some strange reason, people used to think all kinds of weeds, roots, bark of trees and the like would cure warts, flatulence, stop nose bleeds and anything else pertaining to an illness. Yes, science has found some wild growing things to be a cure for many diseases and without them we might all go off the deep end. However, smelling asafetida would burn the hairs off the top of toes and send the gag reflux into a tailspin. It is obnoxious! Whoever decided to use this concoction must have been on a big binge or wasn't able to smell the odiferous, offending scent. Remember the science class and those reeking odors? The ones making the hair stand up or curl on its own? Asafetida is one of those, "gag me with a stick," I am out of here because I need air from this "Devil's Dung."   Asafetida gets its name from a ferula, which is a mega sized fennel species. Deriving from the Persian aza, meaning mastic or resin, and foetidus (Latin for stinking), it is a gum exuded from the sap of the roots and stem of the ferula. Alexander the Great was known to have carried this "stink finger" west in 4 BC. Ancient Rome used this as a spice (go figure... no wonder Rome burned while Nero fiddled) and some singers, during this reign, would slather asafetida with butter in order to enhance their singing qualities. Believe it or not, asafetida was supposedly known as a prescription for asthma, whooping cough, bronchitis, and other respiratory ailments. In the Wild West, some people thought it would cure hysteria and if mixed with other ingredients would cure alcoholism. Phooey! All it did was choke people to death.

All of this brought to mind a girl I went to school with at Sophia Meyer. We were in the fourth grade and each time I passed her my eyes burned. She was a pretty girl, but so help me Hanna, she stayed several arms length from anyone. Her desk was in the back of the room near a window that stayed partially open even during the winter. Our teacher's desk, angled in a corner near the front of the windows, was a bull's eye target for downwind, or should I say upwind nasal contact? It was not uncommon to hear the teacher slam her chair backwards as she dashed toward the hallway for a gulp of fresh air.

Several weeks of unending torture, I was bound and determined to find out why she was so odiferous. We were outside near an old iron bar used for turning summersaults. Pulling a clothespin from my slacks pocket, I pinched my nose with it and headed in her direction. Trouble is, I had to breathe through my mouth and the taste from the odor was not palatable. Speaking in a very nasal tone, I proceeded to ask her why she stank. Was I being rude? No. I really wanted to be her friend but until I could get close enough to her to find out why she had no friends, I had to take the chance.

I watched as she pulled a long dirty string from around her neck. Attached to it was a piece of cotton material full of the most putrid, smelly, stink bombs I ever smelled. It smelled like a million rotten, sulfuric eggs doused in a keg of rancid onions. I asked her what the heck it was and why she had it strapped to her body like a long lost friend. Couldn't she get rid of it? She told me it was asafetida and she couldn't take it from around her neck because it kept her from getting sick. It was to ward off germs. I told her what she said was a bunch of horse feathers and all she was doing was making all of us sick. Then I asked her how she knew she would get sick if she took it off. Her reply was, "My nose will bleed." Naturally, I said, "I don't believe it. It's a crock of bologna. Prove it to me. I want to see your nose bleed."

As she reached for the string and raised the bag of gunk over her head, nothing happened. Without warning, her nose began to bleed. It was the weirdest thing I ever saw and to think a bag of icky junk around a neck could ward off a nose bleed was more than I could fathom. A few minutes after she held her head backwards, her nose stopped bleeding, and the bag of asafetida went back around her neck.

Now, I am not one to believe in hocus pocus or any kind of float-me-in-the-air kind of magic. Her bag of asafetida, whether it was psychological or not, or if she whacked herself in the nose when I wasn't looking, continued to be her friend. She was content.

It was a strange school year. It was my first and last encounter with asafetida and the only season to see this girl. I have no idea where she moved but like the nose bleed, she was gone and the window was shut. For me, it opened up a multitude of questions about science and etched a memory of this delicate balance between nature's bounty and theory.

NUMBER 10 WASH TUBS

If you remember the number 10 wash tub, you are in the same generation as me. Slathering yourself with lye soap while sitting in a tub of water, you came out squeaky clean. However, do you know where this type of bathing came into play? The other day my daughter emailed me a tidbit and I would like to expand on the informed history lesson I would just as soon forget. Thank goodness we live in the twenty-first century and not in the 1500's. It's not a pretty picture but some classic lines sprang forth from the living conditions. Is it fact or fiction?

"A bride carries a bouquet." There was a sinister reason the month of June was set aside for brides in the year 1500. It appears, according to the email, May was the month for the yearly bath, yep, not daily bath but yearly bath! By the time June rolled around, everyone began to reek. In order for the bride to cover an odiferous aroma emanating from her and persons in attendance a bouquet of flowers was placed in her hands to thwart unharmonious nasal swill. Thank goodness times have changed.

It brings us to the bath and why the old saying "Don't throw the baby out with the bath water" came to be a well-known catch phrase. The baths, back then, consisted of a large tub filled with hot water. The first person to bathe was the man, the head of the household. He had the opportunity to enjoy the clean hot water and lounged in the tub until the water was tepid. The woman was next in line and by now the water was becoming cooler and dirtier. If they had several children, age was the factor. The eldest child took a dip and then after all the other children had a go at the water the baby took its turn. By the time everyone washed the grit and grime from their bodies, the water was so grungy the baby could get lost or tossed. Now, I wouldn't think it actually happened, but then again, I don't know.

"It's raining cats and dogs" is because of no support under thatched roofs. There was no wood to keep the straw from falling into a house. Small animals, cats, dogs and vermin crawled into the thatched roofs to stay warm. It was their residence. On occasion the roof would become slimy and critters would fall into the room. It's a rather disgusting picture to know a bed, where you are sleeping, would be interrupted with a critter joining you in the dead of night. Believe it or not, canopy beds with high posts came into the picture. It was the only way to keep unwanted guests from "dropping in" unannounced.

How would you like to have a dirt floor? People of wealth were the only ones to afford slate to walk upon, so the term "dirt poor" only applied to those persons whose houses didn't contain elegant pathways. It backfired when the slate became slippery and straw had to be placed beneath their feet to keep them upright. During the winter, the straw became so thick the people had to put a piece of wood in front of the doors to keep the straw inside. This is how and where we got "threshold."

"Peas porridge hot, pea's porridge cold, pea's porridge in the pot nine days old" came about when people cooked in a large container over a fireplace. At night, when the fire went out, the porridge sat in the container. Each day they would add to the existing fixings (mostly vegetables) and stirred the pot till it became so thick it turned into porridge. "To chew the fat" enters the picture when those able to afford pork "brought home the bacon." Sometimes it was added to the porridge. Yuk!

Bread is another story. Ever wonder where "upper crust" derived? Peons or workers got the scorched bottom of the loaf, the family got the middle portion, and the guests, you guessed it, got the upper crust.

You won't have to remind me to never eat from pewter plates because I would be dead as a hammer from all the tomatoes I consume. Those plates were thought to leach out poison, especially when any types of acidic properties are placed upon it, namely tomatoes. Tomatoes were considered poison. If a person drank any type of home brew from a pewter cup, it usually made them so drunk, at times; they were thought to be dead and prepared for burial. Placed in a coffin, some of the imbibed had strings attached to their hands so they could ring a bell to let them know they weren't dead. England, in the 1500's, ran out of places to inter and re-used coffins. They found a lot of the "re-used" coffins with scratch marks inside and actually hired people to sit in a graveyard to listen for a bell. This is where we get the term "dead ringer" and "saved by a bell."

Ummm, five hundred years from now... what will the people think of us and the phrases we coined? Maybe the people of the future will take a gander of a picture found inside a time capsule. They might gasp and say, "What happened to make them so deformed? Their thumbs have knots." They will be so far advanced they won't even know about the BlackBerry computer / text messaging phones / iPods or such.

Waking up, from sleeping in a capsule somewhere in space, they will be too busy punching a button on their foreheads and tweaking their alien noses for reception. Then, they will try to figure out what to do with a number 10 washtub they found floating around in their orbital space. Look out ... there comes a bar of lye soap!

CARDBOARD SLIDES

We certainly weren't wealthy but comfortable in the knowledge that on occasion, money could be spent on a necessary item. Mother and daddy might have had to save for a long time to acquire something, but like any child, I was not privy to their "money business." Mother was frugal and made things last regardless if it was on its last leg and needed to be chucked to the dump.

Way back when, my mother was delighted in getting a new appliance, but since things held together for many years, buying them was not an everyday occurrence. Any kind of refrigerator, stove or freezer would last for years on end because they weren't designed to fall apart when the warranty ceased. When old appliances kept running, like the little pink rabbit wound up on an overcharged battery, the manufacturers got wise and devised a scheme to sell more products. Manufacturers called it "if we don't sell these products, we can't pad our pockets." Sinister plot?

Yes, it was planned obsolescence designed to gouge the consumer's wallet. It is apparent, in this day and age; most new household items blow up, catch on fire, fall apart, have a recall or just stop working one nanosecond after the warranty goes kaput. Maybe it is because USA made products have gone by the wayside or are outsourced to another country. Whichever the case may be, manufacturers know domestic devices are required to maintain a house, so they delight in digging deeper into our pockets, several hundred or thousands of dollars at a time. As they detonate or deteriorate, we chuck them. Where all these old appliances go is beyond me. Sometimes I believe new items are resurrected from junk pile things people threw away many years ago. When I buy a new item they take on an eerie glow because the blush sure looks familiar and the appliance acts the same. It's déjàvu.

I didn't care one iota about the new item mother bought, what it did or how it looked. The appliance belonged to her ... not me, but the large box discarded was earmarked for fun. The cardboard box was the best toy we could hope for because it was thick and would withstand flying down a slope. Most of the lots on Henry Street had a high slope and gave us ample room to ski (as if we had good sense) down the rough terrain. At the front or smaller side of the box, we would punch a hole, push a heavy duty rope through it and use it as a steering wheel. The box had a mind of its own and the makeshift steering wheel didn't help one bit in making the stupid thing to go straight. Then, as kids gathered to have a go at the ski slope, several of us would sit, front to back with legs secured around the child immediately in front of the other, and with a good shove we would sail down the hill. It didn't matter if the grass was dry or if it caught fire from friction, we would play for hours using the cardboard box as a sled. Lucky for us, everyone had a water hose handy.

If the box had an unusual amount of wear from many trips down the hill, we would cut it into disks and use them sort of like a Frisbee. If truth was known, we invented the Frisbee but didn't have sense enough to know how to patent it. Oh well, que será, será. Many times the box was used as a playhouse as we cut out windows and put red crepe paper on the top for a roof. On rainy days, if it wasn't raining cats and dogs, we had picnics inside them. Caught off guard when there was a deluge we might find ourselves at the bottom of the hill if the water flowed too rapidly. When the box disintegrated, we'd traipse to Matlock's Grocery Store on Lafayette Street and tell the owners, Guy or Jewell, we needed a box. Mr. Matlock would look at us and laugh because he always knew when we had been sailing down a hill. I guess it was because we had dirt all over our faces and skinned knees. Jewell would give him a nudge and nod toward the back of the store. "Why, I bet we can find one. It may not be a big box but you kids are small and I reckon it will do. I bet you need a bottle of chocolate water to cool off, don't you?" I can never remember a time when he didn't offer me my favorite cold drink but I do remember not having two cents to buy it. Most times, he'd pat me on the head and say, "This one is on the house." With Mr. Matlock and Jewell at the helm, we never ran out of a supply of boxes or chocolate water.

    The other day I drove past my old home place, neighborhood houses and the ghost of Matlock's Grocery Store. The grocery store was gone and only a memory stood in its place. Somehow, the home place didn't seem as enormous as I remembered. Grass was growing where our sleds made ruts and the slopes–those death defying slopes–weren't there. Some of the massive trees were gone–no tire swings. No large rocks jutted upward–no King of the Mountain. The best thing I saw was ghosts of the past–children having fun–on a cardboard box.

BLACK-EYE PEAS TRADITION

The other day when I was trying to remember the name of the gentleman on Garrison Avenue that I mentioned in my last story, I phoned various people "in the know." Unfortunately, none of them remembered his name. However, I did get a great, fun to search question from Mrs. Bell about black-eye peas. Actually, she said some of her family frowned or did not understand the importance of eating black-eye peas on New Year's Day.

Eating the traditional black-eye peas, hog jowl, collard greens, cornbread and potatoes goes back a long way. Believe it or not, eating black-eye peas were cultivated in pre-historic times. In China and India they are thought to be a relative of the mung bean and ancient Romans and Greeks called them chickpeas. Then, West African slaves brought them to the West Indies. From there, the pea was brought to the Southern United States, somewhere around 1600. During the 1700's, the Carolinas and Florida had most cultivations. During the Civil War when Sherman's troops pillaged everything in sight and confiscated people's food, they thought the peas, growing in the fields, were not worth anything. Since the peas and other field crops were originally grown for livestock, the troops passed them off as worthless. The slaves and Confederate South ate the "field peas" and animal fodder to survive. After the American Revolution, the state of Virginia grew them in abundance. The pea was so popular it wound up in Texas and around the country.

The pea is subspecies cowpea and is a bean. Various languages refer to it as lobia, ChawLie, or black-eye bean. It is a legume long standing from Washington Carver who was wise to know the pea puts nitrogen back into the soil while in its growing state and after its harvesting. Tilling under the pea's foliage helped the farmer add mulch to used soil. Farmers know to rotate the crops to prevent nematodes. The blossom of the pea is a bonus as bees pollinate and produce honey from its nectar. It seems the lowly pea is abundant in nutrition and nitrogen and survived, in spite of a war to extract. Today, we are fortunate to have the tiny little pea (bean) to enjoy as a tradition and everyday meals.

Eating traditional foods for good luck is nothing new. The Babylonians said if good luck symbols are available, one should partake of the foods. Rosh Hashanna, the Jewish New Year, falling on the seventh month and recorded in Leviticus 23:24 "Speak unto the children of Israel, saying: In the seventh month, in the first day of the month, shall be a solemn rest unto you, a memorial proclaimed with the blast of horns, a holy convocation." Rosh Hashanna meals include honey and apples and some type of meat from the head of a fish or animal to represent the "head" of the year. Different communities ate different foods. Spinach, leeks, black-eye beans, gourds and dates are recorded in the Talmud. Even way back then and now, Hebrews recite prayers, (Yehi Ratson- meaning May it be your will), over foods as a symbolic gesture for the beginning of their New Year.

Eating black-eye peas on the first day of a New Year is thought of as being a good luck symbol to bring prosperity. In the United States, the practice of eating black-eye peas began with Sephardi Jews when they came to Georgia in 1730's. The practice of eating peas was adopted by non-Jews around the time of the American Civil War. Many areas of the United States began eating the peas as a symbol of good luck. They are cooked in various ways, according to geographical locations. Not everyone eats the same thing and some people will gag at the thought of eating jowl. Dried black-eye peas (beans) swell to twice their size when cooked and are thought of as prosperity. Some people will forgo the collards for mustard or turnip greens and they represent money. Hog jowl or ham symbolizes a positive movement forward since all pigs root "forward" when they eat. Cornbread and potatoes, I believe, were thrown in with the meal to add more substance and go further when families were large.

If the little pea could survive through battle, then I suppose it is lucky as it prospered and continues to grow. Because people during the war survived on its properties, they were considered lucky. So, Betty, tell your family while they are eating the good luck meal, they can pass down this little bit of information to their children who will probably snarl their nose at the humble little black-eye pea. As for my family, (yes, my kids snarled, too), we always eat the delicious black-eye peas, greens and jowl. Throw in a chunk of cornbread…how lucky can you get?

DANGED OLD GREMLINS

Why is it that when you think things are going smooth, something gets in the way? Is it to slow us down to make us think? Great balls of fire, my brain hurts from so much thinking, sometimes I can't see straight. You think every angle has been thoroughly honed and smoothed out with two hundred grit sandpaper. Then, all of a sudden and without warning, a hunk of wood juts up in the air like the ground gave birth to it. Ye, Gods, give me a break!

Honestly, though, I think it is goober green gremlins hovering like saber toothed tigers to take a chunk out of us when we least expect it. They hide in crevasses, under the bed, inside cabinets and car hoods. My little gremlins pretend everything is running like a well oiled machine and sneak up behind me. Even though my kids tell me I have eyes in the back of my head, it doesn't help me one iota. Gremlins are colorless apparitions but I know what they look like. Dastardly little devils, they are, grinning from ear to ear with menacing fangs, furry horned ears, whiskers with barbs and evil blood shot purple eyes.

They wait until the last minute to spring forth with a hissing "gotcha" and laugh like hyenas to curdle your blood. If your gremlins are like mine, they wear sneakers so you can't hear them. They tip toe through and around the tulips until they have a clear shot. WHAM! They smack you in the head with those steel toed sneakers until you are senseless. You wind up with a jellybean brain and your body looks like black pudding from a massive pounding. I'm telling you, it is not pretty!

In 1973, Forrest Saffeels, a structural engineer by education and carpenter by trade, custom built our house. It was not pretentious but a house our family could live in and enjoy. The cabinets were built on site and have served me well for all these many years. I have had no complaints. Within this period of time, we have had two freezer-less refrigerators with ice makers. I loved them because they allowed me to have ample room inside for preparation of large family meals. Several microwaves have graced my countertops and gone to the great garbage heaps in the sky. Two drop in ranges and two dishwashers have aided me in my kitchen routine. I have been blissfully happy. Enter those blasted gremlins! My refrigerator decided to leak so Dan and I trekked to the store to purchase another one. Nope, the freezer-less are not produced. Hang it all, we looked at so many side-by-side, top and bottom freezer, ice makers that take up too much space contraptions that if I see another one it will be too soon. Stop looking, I am bleary eyed and ticked off!

Dan said, "Let's do a remodel." I agreed. Now it meant the gremlins were about to strike. Not one at a time, mind you, but the whole damned lot of them. A gas range comes in so many different styles it is like looking at a boxed cereal aisle and all you want is oatmeal. Bells and whistles decorate those things like diamonds on freight trains. Then I look at dishwashers with baskets so small, it will not hold anything bigger than a bikini bra. Here come the gremlins in mass force! It is an all out war. Lo and behold, the microwave sitting on my countertop arced and spit fire. It was a goner. Yep, it was back to the store for a microwave.

I selected one for over the stove installation. Big mistake! When we un-wrapped it and put it on the counter to use temporarily, it engulfed the whole kitchen. I went nuts! It was a gargantuan albatross disguised as a gremlin. Reading the three page instructions for use (no manual...stupid if you ask me not to include a book), I knew right away I was in trouble. That idiot thing would blow up the first rattle out of the box, especially when I can vegetables all summer long. Steam would fry that sucker and I would have holes the size of Manhattan in my new tiles. Wrap, wrap, wrap…back to the store it went. I killed one gremlin…one hundred to go and the battle was raging.

It is time for countertop selection. Since 1973, I have had laminate countertops. I selected a different color and design for "my" kitchen. I agreed to look at granite but the angst inside me from gremlins poking me in the side was becoming insurmountable. Irritation was setting in at a rapid rate. I put a slab of granite (my selection) in the car to go match the tile backsplash. Looking at tile to match the slab was unbearable. It looked as though the combination of tile and granite was the color of puke gruel. It was time to go home…I was sick to my stomach. As I looked at the small slab of granite sitting on the passenger seat of my car, my foot kept ramming in the carburetor and disgust flew from my nostrils. The slab of granite kept getting larger and busier and I hated it. At that moment, I killed some more gremlins as I decided once and for all I did not want granite. Granite is forever, laminate is not! I am a simple person with simple needs. I do not need fancy things to make me happy. After doing monumental research of appliance ratings from consumer reports, burning gasoline and having ring-tailed tooter fits from hair snatching gremlins; my kitchen will be completed.

Where is Hopkins' Furniture and Appliance Store when I need them most? GONE! I remember a time and place when things were simple and Hopkins was there for our appliance and furniture needs. At that time, everyone bought the same type practical products. They were not status symbols or upped re-sale values. Fancy things only applied to the elite as common folk were happy with what they had or could afford. Color me common but I will guarantee you one thing…common or elite…we all have gremlins!

CALGON, TAKE ME AWAY

This has nothing to do with do you remember but for me, the memory will be a lasting reminder of what it is like to do without amenities we take for granted. For all you women out there take heed. For all you men out there it could apply to you, too! Start four months in advance cleaning out stuff if you are planning some type of remodel. It will relieve you of hurry up, get me a moving, too late now, I am crazy as a goose in a hail storm syndrome.

The last month or so, it has been topsy-turvy around our household. As I told you in one of my stories, we were doing a complete remodel of our kitchen. Well, hold on to your latisibles (if you don't know what that means, listen to Brother Dave Gardner and his classic motorcycle story) because doing any type of re-do is one of the most horrific things you can encounter.

You will hang on for the ride of your life. I am not sure my stomach, aching bones and our little dog gone ballistic can endure another remodel. It started with ripping out my existence. By that I mean, my beloved old kitchen…a kitchen that knew me and I knew it. For almost forty years, we were one in my rituals. It did not complain if I spilled something or shut a door or drawer a little too hard.

As I removed the contents of the cabinets, my mothers, grandmothers and Dan's mother and grandmothers' possessions, along with mine spilled over as that of a grand waterfall of beautiful memories. Each item, too dear to part with, pulled passionate thoughts of how their hands caressed and used those items. Inside banana boxes they went and sat in a spare bedroom until time for removal. In fact, two bedrooms and the living room were crammed packed with things coming from my cabinets. Banana boxes sat everywhere and towel covered bedspreads caught leftovers. If my house were to tilt from the weight of the masses, it would slide into the Arkansas River. It was not too bad until I began hunting for a specific item.

First went the dishwasher, then the stove. The refrigerator was moved to the garage for secondary use and sat near its counterparts. Their vacancy, inside the house, meant this was a day to remember. One by one, a cabinet gave up its ghost, exposing its naked and shell less cavity to the cabinet nearby. Nails gripped the wall unwilling to release the fondness for their partners. Some cabinets, reluctant to release their hold, had to be destroyed. They went to the back yard destined for the landfill. Those other cabinets who did not want a sledge hammer attacking its exterior came out with little effort. They had the pleasure of joining the appliances in the garage and would be re-cycled in my son's utility room.

As I walked into the garage, the appliances appeared sad and I had bittersweet thoughts of turning them loose. My electric stove burned out units if I did too much canning and it groaned, on occasion, if a pot was too heavy. It waited, though, until I replaced one of its elements. It never set off smoke alarms! My dishwasher was my right hand when dirty dishes accumulated through family meals. Not to worry as they, along with the refrigerator, would be put to good use. They were donated to the Habitat for Humanity Restore in Fort Smith. Someone will be happy to have these still good, useable appliances.

Now we are without cooking appliances. Resourceful, the BBQ grill, tinfoil, hamburger meat made into patties and seasoned, frozen vegetables came to our rescue. Pile all of it into one large tinfoil tray, cook till meat is done and it will satisfy a growling stomach. Tastes good too!

Eureka, the new cabinets arrived. Now, I am not talking Cadillac cabinets as they are on the line of a Mercedes or Lamborghini. Dennis and Dickie Spahn and employees Roger Miller and shop foreman, Ted Johnston, outdid themselves and the cabinets are beautiful. To the ceiling, linen white cabinets hang proudly and are a far cry from the oak, faded out color from so much scrubbing. It is so bright in my kitchen I do not need overhead light. New backsplash was installed by Tate Young and it is beautiful. Then it was time for the appliances. Van Buren Building Inspector, David Martin, gave my kitchen his approval.

It is like I am walking into someone else's kitchen. It does not know me and I do not know it. Putting everything back into its proper place took some thought. Where something used to be in a cabinet, is no more. You have to hunt as these new cabinets are not configured like the old ones. The new refrigerator is wonderful but still not to my liking. It took me several attempts to organize arrangement for condiments. Where a large container of food will go is beyond me. I guess it will be frozen. My new gas range tested my patience! Gas and electric ranges are so far apart in heat that it will take me awhile to put this stove in proper perspective. I am boss and what I say goes! Burning off the "new" sat off the smoke detector two times and scared the blasted beejeebers out of me.

The kitchen is great but now it is time for the den re-do. All furniture is out, walls cleared, Terry Syrock and his group of painters are here, the paint stinks to high heaven, I am getting a major headache and I have two choices…go outside and let the pollen turn my hair puce green or stay in the office and be asphyxiated. The den is gorgeous but need I say more…yep…Calgon, take me away!

DAYLIGHT SAVINGS TIME

Good grief, Benjamin Franklin had too much time on his hands! Pun intended. Famed for the notable proverb, "Early to bed, and early to rise, makes a man healthy, wealthy, and wise" did not take into consideration how cranky, slothful, and sleepy it makes mortal man. This was in 1784. He thought the Parisians were using too many candles declaring they get out of bed at an early hour to economize and utilize daylight. Although it was a satire, the Parisians kept shutters closed and Franklin thought they needed to tax the closed shutters and candles. Franklin even thought all the church bells needed to peal to rattle them out of bed and if that did not work, cannons should be fired at sunrise. Holy mackerel…imagine being shaken to the core by cannon fire because if Franklin was awake, everyone else should follow suit.

It was not Franklin who proposed DST as eighteenth century Europe did not keep schedules. DST was proposed in 1895 by George Vernon Hudson. He was an entomologist but worked day shifts. When he found out that two extra hours of daylight allowed him more time to collect bugs, he drafted a letter to the Wellington Philosophical Society explaining the necessity of the two-hour daylight saving shift.

Then someone else jumped on the bandwagon. In 1905, an avid golfer named William Willett, who was out for a leisurely ride before breakfast, decided he did not like to cut his golfing short at dusk. He felt, while he was enjoying the additional hours of sunlight, the Londoners' who slept too much during the summer hours needed to wake up. It did not stop there!

Enter World War I. Britain and other European countries, in order to cut back on the use of coal during the conflict of war, adopted Willett's day light savings. It was not until 1918 that the United States came aboard. Since then, many things changed. It was not a popular thing and Congress, after WWI, abolished it. President Woodrow Wilson's veto was overridden. Some states kept it as an option until WWII when President Franklin Roosevelt declared a year round DST in 1942. "War Time" DST stayed in place until 1942 and lasted until 1945. DST was enacted to save on fuel and energy. It seems from September 1945 (after the war) to 1966, there was no federal law to regulate DST so many states could choose if they wanted to remain within this time change.

Move forward, fall backward is one of those things that I would rather split the difference and leave the clocks alone forever and ever, amen! It can't happen because to do so would change mean times all over the world. Communications, travel via rail, air and other public transit would have to change drastically to accommodate world times. Some people say we get a free extra hour but that is hogwash. There are only 24 hours in a day and regardless of how many times we mess with those hands on the clock, it will not change. Poor little school kids are either standing in the dark to go to school in the spring or running like the dickens to get home before it gets dark in the winter. DST messes with the brain…either you are sleepy or got too much sleep. Some clocks aren't changed and then you drive like mad to get to the job on time.

This year was the pits for me. Dan had already tilled the garden and mowed up leaves to put on our compost pile. Other things beckoned his attention and he left me to do what I wanted to do outside. It was a beautiful Saturday and time to dig in the dirt to eradicate weeds. I was having a heyday, heave hoeing unwanted growth inside my flowerbeds. Piles of leaves, weeds and sticks mounded up like the showdown at OK Corral and my shovel, hoe and rake was my pistol keeping things under control.

Unfortunately, I needed water...tons of water as the wind was parching me like the Sahara.

As I stepped inside the den, my brain went out of control. I ran as fast as I could to put away the weeding equipment, gloves and work shoes. I was fuming because I did not want to stop working but time had slipped away from me. The clock told me it was after 5:00 p.m. and time to prepare our evening meal. Oh, joy! I began slinging stuff together for burgers. Slicing tomatoes, pickles and all the junk a person piles on a hamburger bun. It was so nice outside; I asked Dan if he would grill the burgers. "Why right now?" he said. "Can't it wait awhile?" "Aren't you hungry?" I asked him with a disgusted sigh. "No." he popped off in a leave me alone attitude.

Now I was downright mad. I put up all my working equipment to fix our meal and he sat there with a smug smirk on his face. I snapped "Well, when do you plan on eating...midnight? It is almost six o'clock." "No, it isn't." A smart-alecky grin smeared across his face, "I already turned the clocks forward one hour!" I stomped away while he sat there braying like the maniacal donkey on Hee-Haw.

Dang it all, I was teed off in a big way. Dan and those blasted clocks messed with my brain, screwed up one hour of working outside and would make me go to bed one hour earlier than I intended. All of our Saturday evening British sitcoms would be off sync with the clocks, I would have to glue my eyes shut to go to sleep and wake up one hour later the next morning just to stay ahead of my brain. I did not know if I was coming or going or what time it was. I will stay that way until someone says to change the danged clocks backward the way they were…all for the extra hour they say is free.

In our household, DST means…Dan screwed with the time!

VAN BUREN POST OFFICE / GENE MARTIN

The date was November 1, 1935. It would be a crowning victory for the citizens of Van Buren to have a new post office. The site chosen was a small plot of land on the corner of Seventh and Webster Streets. Construction would have to wait until Postal engineer R.J. Evans came to town to survey the proposed site. It was preliminary survey work until the bids were secure. Not until March 13, 1936 were the plans completed. Even though the low bidder was Charles H. Barnes of Logansport, IN, it appeared his bid and all the others were rejected by the postal service in July because they were deemed too high. Again, in August and September, Barnes resubmitted his bid of $54,223. It was accepted. The post office would begin construction.

The employees and carriers would have the finest area to rest between the off working hours. A beautiful white mezzanine floor would decorate that area. Grand opening for the Van Buren Post Office was in 1937. Funds, in the amount of $590, were set aside in the bid allocating for an original 12' x 5' mural. It would be placed over the postmaster's door. Section Chief Edward B. Rowan requested artist E. Martin Hennings of Taos, NM to submit an original design to adorn the interior of the post office. After a multitude of submitted sketches, either too disturbing, sweet, and not convincing enough to portray the men as virile for the pioneer lifestyle, rejections mounted. The color was off, characters depicting the scene were not suitable, faces were forlorn or too happy seemed to delay progress.

    Finally, in 1940, after many sketches and earnest money paid to Mr. Hennings, the oil on canvas mural was completed. Mr. Hennings' wife and daughter posed for the females and a Mexican man, Americanized in facial features, served as a model for the male head of the household figure. The depiction of the mural shows a pioneer family with a covered wagon, driven by oxen, as they travel west along the Arkansas River. Due to dangerous situations they must have encountered along their perilous journey they had to hope and pray of better things to come. As Mr. Hennings' renderings settled this beautiful family in Van Buren, the title was "The Chosen Site."

Mr. Hennings was born on February 5, 1886 in the town of Pennsgrove, NJ. His training in oils was from the Art Institute of Chicago and the National Academy of Munich. Expertise in oils allowed him to receive many awards and prizes and his works hangs in museums across New Mexico and the United States. He passed away in 1956. Van Buren's legacy from Mr. Hennings is the commissioned artwork for our town.

The person I knew best at the Van Buren Post Office was Marion Eugene "Gene" Martin. I always saw him in the post office but it wasn't until 1962, that I really got to know him. He and his family attended St. John's United Methodist Church, the church where Dan and I were married. It was an honor to know his wife, Peggy, who passed away on April 10, 2007. Their children are Peggy, Marian, Charlie, Tom and David (Van Buren Building Inspector).

In 1935, Mr. Martin was paid sixty-five cents an hour as a substitute clerk and $2100 a year in 1942. Seeing the need to help our country during the war, he was furloughed from the postal service and joined the United States Navy in 1942. When the navy realized Mr. Martin was astute in postal service, they put him to work in mail service. During this time, Philadelphia, PA native, Margaret "Peggy" Jardel, a Wave, was stationed at Great Lakes Naval Station in Chicago, IL.

The naval base is where he and Peggy first met. In 1945 when the war was over, Mr. Martin and his wife Peggy returned to Van Buren. Mr. Martin returned to his duties at the post office and was made Assistant Postmaster in 1946 by Postmaster E.W. Deering. His pay was $3300.00 a year.

In 1962, President John F. Kennedy appointed Mr. Martin postmaster of Van Buren, AR. President Kennedy's signature to the certificate would not come to fruition due to his assassination by Lee Harvey Oswald. Mr. Martin's certificate was then signed by President Lyndon B. Johnson. For twenty-seven years his duty was that of substitute and regular clerk, and assistant postmaster and nineteen years postmaster. Mr. Martin served the city of Van Buren a total of forty-six years.

Mr. Martin was one of a kind. Always happy, he greeted everyone in Van Buren and went above and beyond the call of duty to assist his patrons. Many times he took mail to people on Sunday even though he was not bound to do so. He realized delivering mail or packages, from loved ones far away from their families, would give his patrons an uplifting spirit.

The downtown post office still serves the community and the mural over Mr. Martin's office remains. The mural's title, "The Chosen Site", is a fitting reminder of how one man, Marion Eugene

"Gene" Martin who passed away on December 19, 1982, and his "chosen" career served this city. Mr. Martin may be gone from this earth but his spirit, not forgotten, still walks the mezzanine floors in the Van Buren Post Office.

MOTHER'S OLD TIME REMEDIES

It's flu season! A time when hacking coughs send you into a tailspin, fever makes your head woozy; a stuffy nose makes you sound like you are stuck in a barrel, your eyes water when you sneeze, the sight of food makes you reel and if you drink one more glass of water it will make you gag.

Raise your hand if you remember being sick as a junkyard dog and your mom slapped Ben Gay, mentholated rub, or a mixture of turpentine and lard (hog fat) on your chest. I can't raise enough hands or feet. Those smelly rubs were enough to choke a horse and the only thing it did was make me stink. It was bad enough to see the round blue jar or tube of blistering icky stuff but when mother put a hot towel over the smarmy junk, I could almost see fumes dance in the air. Either one of the powerful medicines made the eyes water while it burned the airs out of the nose. It knocked you out cold because you couldn't hold your eyes open with a wide tooth comb. Turpentine and hog fat was even worse. The sensation in feeling the slimy, greasy goop was too much! Not only that, you couldn't wash the stench off your body with a barrel of lye soap. Not to worry, though, everyone at school stank like you did.

So much for flu and rub on gunk. Let's talk about a nose bleed or a cut on the hand or foot. Mother swore by heaven and earth on a certain home remedy. I have to admit, it worked but wasn't the best looking poultice. Ye Gods, it reminded me of a giant tick. Remember the old space heaters… you know, the kind sitting in the corner of a room billowing out carbon monoxide fumes? Matches would lay on the corner of the heater…remember those little stick matches scorched from blazing heat? How about the ring of black soot stuck to the ceiling from its exhaust? Remember when you didn't have an over head exhaust fan over the cook stove? Well, combine the space heater and grease components of cooking food and it results in cobwebs. Yeah, I said cobwebs, those black stringy things hanging from the ceiling…the kind of things giving a kid a nightmare because they swear giant spiders are hanging on the ends. It never failed but I was the recipient of one of those blasted, dust filled greasy cobwebs. So help me, every time mother saw me with a little cut or nose bleed, she would take a single broom straw, twist one of those hanging nightmares, wad it up in a ball and make me hold it on my cut. Sometimes I walked around with so many cobwebs stuck to my arms and legs; I looked like I had some kind of plague. Another remedy she used was coal oil. We always had a jar of that stuff on hand for major cuts. Stick your foot in a pan of it and it was supposed to prevent blood poisoning making streaks up your legs. If a cut was deep, she packed sugar into the wound. I don't know how it worked but it did.

Now that we know about the flu and cobwebs, let's move on to a sore throat. I never told mother when I had a sore throat…one time was enough! Her remedy for a sore throat should have been classified as a secret…never to be written down in the annals of Joyce's science, let alone in Joyce's mouth. It was the most hideous concoction. She never could find a small onion; it had to be a large one. She would mince the onion and put it in a cup of water and simmer over low heat. When it turned into mush, somewhat like slushy snow, she strained it and set it aside until cool. Add a dash of garlic and ginger and a tablespoon of lemon juice … what the hell, go ahead and add two tablespoons of lemon juice…it won't do anything but make you pucker. Throw in a hand full of lemon seeds for good measure! It helped knock holes in the tonsils so the onion juice would go further in the throat. The first time mother used this on me was the last time. She had to coax me into trying the nasty gargle and when it hit my mouth and tonsils, it killed any kind of germ lurking within ten feet of my body. I smelled worse than Gertie's drawers for a solid week and reeked like something the cat wouldn't bury. Today, every time I pick up an onion, I hear mother say, 'Ah, it's just a little bit of onion; it will help your sore throat.'

If I had an earache she blew cigarette smoke inside my ears. If my stomach hurt a tablespoon of mustard or fourth cup of pickle juice did the trick. I still use this practice for an upset stomach as it really works. My all time favorite was if I had a stye on my eye because it allowed me to stay up late at night. At midnight, she would walk with me to the corner. It had to be a four way stop. I had to walk backwards to the center of the area and repeat this little ditty...four times. "Stye, stye, leave my eye and go to the next one passing by." Then when my mantra was complete, I had to walk backward, toward mother, with the good eye shut. I felt the fool doing what she told me to do but it worked. Perhaps, though, it was ready to heal. Mother's hot compress, clamped to the eye with the force of a vice, would pop a boil on a bull. It was strange, after the midnight trek, the next morning the stye would be gone. Every day, thereafter, my eyes squinted at those walking on the sidewalk. I wanted to see who caught my stye. I wouldn't look them straight in the eye because I didn't want them to give it back to me. It was a vicious circle.

Mother was a rare breed and full of so many home remedies, it is a wonder I made it through puberty. Funny thing is…after all these years and practicing her remedies, I am my mother. Every time I look in the mirror, I see her but if I have a sore throat…I tell her an emphatic…no onions!

PICKETT HILL & CROWN CEMETERY

Everyone who has lived in Van Buren for any length of time knows the words Pickett (sometimes spelled Picket) Hill. How many of you know how or when it got its name and where it is located? Way back in 1820, a river port, called Phillips Landing was owned by Revolutionary War veteran James Phillips and his two sons, Daniel and Thomas. The Phillips' also established the first post office in 1831. Thomas Phillips was the postmaster.

Then in 1836, John Drennen and his brother-in-law, David Thompson (from Tennessee) opened up a ferry service and purchased Phillips Landing. Drennen was appointed postmaster and platted out the streets in Van Buren. When Van Buren became a county seat in 1838 the courthouse land, where it now stands, was donated to the city by Mr. Drennen. Our town was incorporated in 1845.

During the gold rush of 1849, Van Buren was already a bustling, thriving town due in part to the major "highway" called the river. It provided many gold rush enthusiasts and traders a venue to lade cargo. Can you imagine steamboats chugging up and down the river carrying goods from major cities such as Ohio and Louisiana or Van Buren being a smuggling center for whiskey to the Cherokees? Slavery in the state of Arkansas ran rampant as prosperity took its hold. Some 'players' of Van Buren's society boasted of their wealth and slaves but slavery was about to cease. Abraham Lincoln's election in 1860 brought a halt to expanding slavery and threw eleven southern states (Arkansas included) into declaring they would sever ties with the United States. This was a prelude to Pickett Hill's moniker and a cemetery, Crown Hill, located at the end of 25th Street in Van Buren.

It's Civil War time–a time for bloody battle to end the era of slavery. Families were pitted against each other and the north and south would be split apart by differences of opinion and bitterness. After two battles, around 8,000 Cain Hill Union troops, out of Washington County, marched on and captured Van Buren in 1862. A total of nine military Civil War exercises were seen in Van Buren between the years 1861-1865. Union troops destroyed virtually everything in Van Buren: courthouse records, steamboats, thousands of bushels of corn, printing presses and houses and they took prisoners of war. Some wealthy landowners' homes were seized and used for Union military.

Rioting, murders and mayhem was at an all time high and all public services such as trials and lawsuits were not heard and taxes were not collected. Everything came to a standstill as chaos choked prosperity to an end. Van Buren was occupied for two years. During these years, Civil War Federal guards, (called pickets), used the land on Pickett Hill as an encampment. Although the knoll was not extremely high, it gave views to the Arkansas River bottom lands as well as flatlands surrounding the area. Guards, made up of two sergeants, four corporals, one lieutenant, and forty privates from regimental areas were always on duty. Forming a ragged line (much like a picket fence) around the main camp, they were accountable for securing the area. For any infantryman, the work was perilous as they were subject to direct sniper fire. Some might argue Pickett Hill was named after Major General George Pickett and troops from Lieutenant A.P. Hill's Third Corps. Your guess is as good as mine as I did not live through that era.

By 1868 when reconstruction began to pull the south out of a quagmire, railroads were already into play. The correlation between the Civil War, railroads and Pickett Hill was when Choctaw, Oklahoma and Gulf Railroad bought the Little Rock and Memphis Railroad and subsequently became known as Chicago, Rock Island and Pacific Railroad. It seems fitting Pickett Hill, used during the Civil War, would be used once again at the beginning of World War II.

As a small training facility, Pickett Hill (then called Camp Walter Johnson) was where soldiers were trained in how to operate seized railroads in enemy territory. However, the Department of War needed more land to train its soldiers and purchased thirty-five acres of estate land from the widow of Dr. Lucas Giles. This land, Pickett Hill where the Crawford County Memorial Hospital now sits, would be called Camp Jesse Turner in honor of his justice on the Arkansas Supreme Court. It is ironic that a Civil War to abolish slavery would determine the outcome of Van Buren's prosperity and quite possibly, great-great grandchildren of those enslaved would come to its rescue. In 1943, 400 African-American soldiers would be bivouacked on Pickett Hill to help all the people in Van Buren's flooded area prepare for fall planting. Camp Jesse Turner, with the help of African-American men, provided housing and assistance to all the families whose homes and land were destroyed in the flood of 1943. A single child was born at the camp and was named Jesse Turner Rutledge. Land was purchased from a Mr. Culver.

The area of Pickett Hill was, at one time, a low income housing district for people of color and Crown Hill Cemetery, once known as Pickett Hill Cemetery, is an African-American Cemetery.

Source:
http://www.flickr.com/photos/sunnybrook100/sets/72157602547523865/

POKE SALAD

Whatever you call it, poke or Polk salad, salet, or pokeweed that grows wild in fields, along streets and forests is one of the best cooked greens I ever tasted. Actually, Poke is considered an herb and can grow up to ten feet tall. It is toxic to mammals, even the leaves. The most poisonous part is the rootstock. Birds eat the berries but because the seeds are so tough, they are eliminated whole.

When I was small, mother and daddy would gather up old flour sacks, load my sister and me in the back seat of the car and head for their favorite "poke" site. It seemed like we drove for hours before we reached Natural Dam. Now that I think about it, it did take hours as mother would yell, "J.D., stop." By the time we got to the intended destination, one flour bag would be filled.

I will never forget mother screaming to high heaven when she came up on a snake. It was not a large snake but it was a rattlesnake. Not to worry though, out came daddy's colt 45 and ka-blooie, the snake was history. Daddy cut off the three buttons and danged near scared mother to death when he pitched them in her lap. He had a sinister side and thoroughly enjoyed hiding the rattles in a paper sack. When someone asked him what he had in the sack, he would laugh and say, "Would you like to look?" Right before the person took a peek; he would rattle the sack and try to hand the sack to the person. He nearly got into fist fights over the rattlesnake buttons.

A friend of daddy's lived up the dirt road near the old rock school on Highway 59. Out in his field, near a fence row, was the largest growth of poke I ever saw. Guarding the field was a huge bull. Making sure our pant legs were secure with rubber bands (cut off circulation) and long sleeved shirts were buttoned to the neck and tightly around the wrist, we would trek off into the field. Mother slathered petroleum jelly on any exposed skin to ward of mosquitoes and chiggers. With a long stick in hand, we would thwack the ground to make critters run. Getting near the fence was easy but made me have second thoughts about sticking my hand near the rock wall that held the fence together. It was catch twenty-two. If we wanted to eat the poke, we picked but old sneaky snake, inside the rocks, was itching to take a bite out of us. I do not know what was worse...the snakes or "Billy Bob" the "I am the king of the walk" bull. You could not turn your back on either one.

Anyway, we never gathered the large leaves or any leaves containing a red or pink color. The roots were never eaten as they are considered highly toxic and can cause severe abdominal cramps and a host of other serious ailments. The small three or four inch high stems growing near the base of a large stalk are what we chose. Those were tender and less toxic than the parent plant. By the time we got home, the petroleum jelly was oozing down our cheeks and seed ticks were crawling on our pant legs.

Washing all those danged poke greens was the pits but using two, number 10 wash tubs did the trick. Mother boiled the greens five times and poured off the water at each successive boil. She always rinsed the greens after each boil. I could smell those greens cook and salivated with the thought of a slab of cornbread, pinto beans and those greens for supper. Daddy liked his greens with scrambled eggs but my all time favorite was greens fried in bacon drippings. I am not advocating any of you eat poke but merely pointing out poke has been a staple in southern cuisine since the Great Depression. During the pioneer years, poke was used as a folk remedy for many ailments and during the Civil War, many letters were written with the pokeberry ink.

For years I have tried to cultivate wild poke but nothing materialized. Either I was not holding my mouth right or I needed to trek to the country or find the green leaves along the roadway. This year was a bonanza. As I began cleaning one of my flowerbeds, tons of small tender poke shoots were immerging from the ground. Last year, I noticed my neighbor left an old stalk to the elements and I hoped he would not see fit to cut it down. Those bright reddish black seeds, adhering to the withering stalk, dropped inside my flowerbed. As I picked the tender shoots, memories of mother and daddy, the Colt 45, rattlesnake buttons, Billy Bob, ticks, chiggers, mosquitoes and petroleum jelly made me burst into laughter.

As I cooked my greens the way mother taught me it was as though she was standing beside me giving motherly instructions. Out of curiosity, I scrambled an egg and added it to my small bowl of greens. I whispered, under my breath, that daddy was right about the combination. It was almost complete, sans one thing…breaking out in hot sweat from daddy's sack of rattlesnake buttons.

I DUNNO!

Funny things you find when you are not searching for them. I found green stamps…you know, those things women collected back in the good old days, tons of keys that did not fit any lock, McDonald's toys from long eaten food and a spattering of other disgusting things. Most women know exactly where they put things and men say you have to think like a woman to find them. The proverbial needle in a haystack is only needed when you cannot find it and then most likely you have to sit down on it to let it make a point. I still did not find what I was looking for…a fever thermometer.

When my kids were small, a fever thermometer was in each of their rooms, as well as, several in each of the bathroom medicine cabinets. It did not take long to find one to check their temperature if they pretended to be sick. However, if their ears turned blood red and they looked at me cross-eyed, they were sick as junk yard dogs. They could only pull the heated wash cloth on the brow; I need to stay home from school trick one or two times. I got wise to the antics when they zipped through the hallway or climbed up the hall wall putting their feet on the ceiling. It took me a while to figure out how feet print wound up on popcorn ceilings and why peanut butter, six feet off the floor, smeared on 1970 wood paneling.

As I said, many thermometers graced my house, all within reach. Sometimes a thermometer wound up where it should not be and it questioned my sanity. Are females destined to be crazy from birth or do we acquire it from giving birth? It was Christmas vacation and a pot of homemade vegetable soup was simmering on the stove. No one was sick so why was an empty thermometer container laying on the counter? As I pondered the question, feeling foreheads as a mother would do, an awful thought crept into my head. No, they would not do it, would they? Squelching the tendency of a mother's gut instinct, I went about my daily routine. The boys were in the kitchen and my daughter was in her bedroom. It got quiet, quieter than I anticipated. As I walked into the kitchen, I was aghast. Both boys were dipping a thermometer into the hotter than hot soup. Pow! The tip blew off and mercury shot into the air. Where did it land? Smack dab in the soup along with tiny glass fragments from the exploding thermometer. My temperature was boiling and I was at my wits end. The boys scattered as I yelled "why did you do what you did." "I dunno," was their answer. I stood there with my mouth gaping. Good grief, what was I to do with all the mercury laden soup? We could not eat it and I could not throw it out the back door for critter consumption. Finally, I ladled it into containers, marked it hazardous and froze it for later disposal. I was thankful when the trash service hauled it away. Yes, I redid the soup, hid the remaining thermometers from myself and watched the kids like a hawk.

The other day, in 107 degree weather, I was colder than an ice cube in a deep freeze. Any way you slice it, one minute cold and the other burning up, made me realize I had a fever. I needed a thermometer. Most times, my inflicted nemesis is from digging in compost with allergies raging at will. So, I shrugged off the unwanted pests and continued with what was at hand. It worked for a while until Dan came down with the same symptoms. Uh, oh…I just did both of us a mischief. My allergies, a.k.a. pneumonia, were transferred to Dan. He went to a doctor and I opted to wait until my good doctor came back from vacation. Thinking all was well with my body; one morning I crawled bleary eyed from the bed and could not walk…literally. My right leg hurt so badly, the pain shot clear up to my brain. For several days I gimped around with a tender buttocks, shin, calf, and muscle spasms. I could not stand up and I could not sit down. As I tried in vain to walk my dog, at one point I thought I would have to get down on all fours and do the baby thing. It did not take too much persuasion to get me to visit my friendly chiropractor, Dr. Kristy Graham. How this small person can wrack a body is beyond comprehension but she does it well. I thought the pain was gone. Not so! Back I went for four acupuncture sessions. It felt marvelous and I began to feel better…until…a charley horse the size of a grapefruit bit into my left calf, did a cantaloupe into my thigh and swelled into a watermelon patch in my butt. Now, I really could not walk, nor gimp. I was in a world of hurt. Bad enough it was but then, trying to sleep became a nightmare. No comfort and then, wham…I pulled a crick in my neck. I became watery eyed, sore throat, cough laden and cold again. Under a thermal blanket I went until I gasped for cold air. Searching for a thermometer was futile. None of those blasted things were anywhere to be found. I gave up the search.

Several days later praying for divine intervention and gritting my teeth in angst determination to win this miserable war, I angled my rear end into my office chair trying to relieve sciatica torture. My fingers worked so I decided to clean out a drawer in my office desk. Peek-a-boo, an elusive mercury laden glass container showed itself. I asked Dan if he knew how it got there. With a shrug, he said, "I dunno." Frustrated, with the family of "I dunno", I threw away the useless green stamps and all the other junk except for the thermometer. Next time, "I dunno" will not be able to baffle me and the thermometer will be at my fingertips. I super glued its cockeyed, little yellow container to the medicine cabinet. This, I know. Pneumonia and "I dunno" are one and the same…both contagious and it takes a royal, ghastly, wigged out pain in the butt to find a thermometer.

SNUFF

Snuff is one of those things that take on different meanings. It can mean examine, to express disdain, snipping off the tip of a candle, or breathing. It can take on a nefarious act of offing someone. Generally speaking, snuff can be a noun, verb or idiom. The stuffy snuff I refer to can knock off your socks and put you in a stupor...a wild eyed, grab on to the nearest tree and hang on for the ride of your life.

Back in the 50's, a small grocery store (name eludes me) was on the southeast corner of Arkansas and Knox Streets. It was a dirty white clapboard sided structure. It had two front doors, much like French doors, but only the one on the right was used to enter. It was held open by a heavy duty rock. A screen door, to keep out flies and mosquitoes, banged to and fro when the wind began to blow. Just to the left of the entryway was a large wood rail used to latch the front doors together when the store was closed. A black wood stove tried to heat the entire store during the winter. There was no air-conditioning during the hot sweltering summer months. The front had a small covered stoop with steep wood steps to walk inside. Most often, when a torrential downpour fell from the heavens, you had to dodge mud puddles. The grocery store was one room with shelves lining the exterior walls. A few baskets of fresh vegetables and weighing scales sat near the counter at the back of the store. Sometimes, during the summer, the front stoop was lined with the vegetables to keep swarming gnats from invading the store. Two doors, one on each side of the rear of the store allowed the proprietor to enter small living quarters. It was a lovely little store.

During these years, Grandma and Grandpa Hawkins lived at the uppermost northern end of Knox Street. To reach their house you had to travel the entire length of Knox Street, a boulder laden dirt road. Sometimes the rocks would be so large a vehicle driver had to try and straddle them or risk puncturing tires. It was precarious because the one lane road had deep ditches on each side and at the base of the hill was a one way rickety wood bridge. You either went into the ditch or banged the underpinning of a car or plowed into a swollen branch when it rained. Take your pick! Walking up and down the steep incline left a lot to be desired, because half way up the hill, a healthy person would be gasping for breath. Couple that with intense heat and dusty terrain you might die of heat exhaustion. It seemed, at one time, construction at the base of Knox Street to install the water tunnel to Fort Smith would collapse the mountain.

My cousin and I enjoyed going to grandma's house. We knew every inch of the backwoods and traipsed all over herrikins deck to avoid the bumpy road. One time we should have listened to our instincts and avoided what we decided to do. Grandma dipped and sniffed snuff! She would put the tip of her little finger inside the can, hold it under her nose and sniff the nasty, hair-sticking powdered tobacco or place a wad under her lower lip. The little grocery store had small tins of the brown substance. The container was as round as a quarter and almost the length of the index finger. A manufactures logo was imprinted on the top. To guarantee freshness, a glued down paper seal guarded its contents. Enter stupidity! Grandma asked us to go buy a can of the nasal congestion, lung choking junk. Why sure, she and I thought it would be an exciting venture as we could stop and watch the construction, listen to the roar of machinery as it deafened our senses, and lollygag along doing whatever we wanted to do. We were going to pick large clusters of Elderberry flowers so we could use them for umbrellas but the construction crew destroyed them. We figured we had been gone long enough to make grandma worry so we went to the grocery store and purchased the coveted tin of grandma's favorite brand of snuff.

On the way home, curiosity got the better of us. What did snuff taste like and could we dip the tip of our pinky fingers into the sneeze provoking stuff? Stupid is as stupid does described us to a "T." Half way up the almost 90 degree road, she and I opened the can of snuff. We were laughing like two hyenas, thinking we were about to pull off a prank grandma would never find out about. Plunk went two little fingers. Sniff and dip went two pug noses. Down on the ground went four knees then two butts. Four eyes turned into eight, then to sixteen and we were hugging the boulders like long lost friends. We were sick as junk yard dogs because we accidently swallowed spit, our eyes were blurry, snuff dripped down our noses and creases of our lips with the force of a waterfall and we began crawling up the hill. We couldn't stand upright without using sticks as canes.

Finally, after two hours of sifogging along, sneezing and gagging we went through grandma's front door. She took one look at us and laughed so hard tears fell from her eyes. How did she know? Well, for the fact we looked like raccoons with well defined eyes and mad dogs frothing at the mouth we denied ever dipping that rotten concoction. If it hadn't been for the ever loving, danged old paper seal on the snuff container giving away our secret, we could have said our dirty faces was the result of dust and sweat.

For me, snuff is nefarious. I classified it as a onetime, gaggy old brown piece of dung, never ever again will I hang on to a boulder in the middle of a road to do a snoot full…it "offed" me on the first pinky dip.

SOUND OF THE WHISTLE

Whistles come in all shapes and sizes. There are dog, game, toy, kettle, cat, wolf, train, lips, police, whistleblower and cannery whistles. Some may make your eardrums go nuts, those you cannot hear but dogs can, kettle whistles when water is boiling, cat and wolf whistles from a male trying to be macho to females, train whistles that seem to be lonesome, puckered lips whistling a tune, police whistles to call attention to someone errant, clean as a whistle, blowing the whistle on wrongdoings, whet the whistle and cannery whistles announcing a shift. You name it; just about anything can have a whistle or use whistle in its moniker.

Whistles go back a long way. How far? It is hard to pinpoint the exact date because a papyrus reed, bone or piece of wood can be used as a whistle. Sources I have read say whistles go back as far as medieval times during the Crusades calling English crossbow men to arms. Rome and Greece used a type of whistle made out of a pipe to keep men in a galley. Pipe whistles, used by boatswain upon naval ships, evolved from the type used in Greece and Rome. These are used to salute dignitaries and issue commands. A modern, regular whistle, the kind we know today, was used in 1878 during a sports event at Nottingham Forest Soccer Club. After this event, a brass whistle, with a small pea inserted inside a hollow chamber, was fashioned by an English toolmaker. He was in awe of how a small pea could generate loud noise when activated by a blast of air. This common whistle known as the "pea" continues to be the largest selling whistle in America.

When I was small, mother taught me how to make a whistle out of ordinary red clay. Henry Street was notorious for the red clumping, stick to your feet when it is wet soil. Water has great difficulty penetrating clay but adding a small amount to a chunk of red clay can be a lot of fun. Now-a-days, you can purchase air drying clay to make most anything, even a whistle.   Mother would shovel a bucket of dry clay and sift it until it had no rocks or pebbles. Pouring it on a clean surface, she made a well in the center and began adding small portions of water until it took on a thick pliable consistency. As she dipped her hands in water, the red clay would wad up as that of a small jack's ball. She stuck her thumb in the center forming it into a small bowl and continued until it looked like a tiny pizza crust. When it was thin she joined all of the outsides together making a smooth round hollow ball. A small twig was used to puncture only the top of the ball on a slant. Then she used a Popsicle stick making a slot near the small hole. It was time to dry the whistle. Sometimes it would whistle other times not. It was a lot of fun but to tell the truth, Tyler's or Sterling's Five and Dime had plastic ones all ready for use.

Daddy knew every train whistle, if they were pulling in or leaving the yard. They are codes using short or long sounds (toots). When stopped, three short toots means a train is backing up or someone is acknowledging a hand signal to back up. Four shorts means to repeat the code, it was not understood or call for signals. Two long, one short, one long means a train is approaching a public crossing. One short, train is approaching a passenger station. One long, train is stopped. If a lot of sounds emitted, it was a warning to people or some kind of animal on the tracks. Daddy always knew which train was on the tracks by these simple whistles or who the engineer was on any given day. He would look at his railroad watch and say,

"She's on time, she's running late or "Joe" must be on sick leave."

The whistle I remember most is from the cannery. Clocks in every house could be set by the blast of the whistle. We always knew when it was noon, when people were getting off work or when it was time for a shift change. I loved the sound as it reverberated through the neighborhood. When it rained, it sounded lonesome as if the end of the sound was searching for a place to stop. For most factories or canneries, the whistle was created by a boiler and whistle or full steam. In the 50's almost every factory had a different sounding whistle. When the whistles went off at the same time, it sounded like a giant pipe organ playing music. It was noisy but beautiful. It meant people were working. Then the whistles ceased. The air did not play music as people punched time clocks. A noon whistle was no longer important.

Some factories still hold to the noon whistle but not in this area. The other day, I heard the most glorious sound. I phoned Allen Canning Co., Bekaert Corporation, Tyson Foods Inc., Arkhola Sand and Gravel, and various other places but it was not their whistle. Doing a search on the internet, I surmise by this quote, "(c) Across the Arkansas Waterway, the draw of the Van Buren Railroad Drawbridge, mile

300.8 at Van Buren, Arkansas, is maintained in the open position except as follows: 1) When a train approaches the bridge, amber lights attached to the bridge begin to flash and *an audible signal on the bridge sounds*. At the end of 10 minutes, the amber light continues to flash; however, the audible signal stops and the draw lowers and locks if the photoelectric boat detection system detects no obstruction under the span. If there is an obstruction, the draw opens to its full height until the obstruction is cleared."

If this is what I heard it was beautiful. For a while, I was transfixed in the past, standing in my childhood front yard, listening to the sound of the whistle.

Source: http://www.gpoaccess.gov/index.html

SULFUR MATCHES

The other day Dan and I were driving to a location. It is eerie how we tune in to each other's thoughts but we do. The same thought crept into our minds at the same time. Drive down North 20th Street. It seemed so strange and lonely without all the houses, houses we knew from a long time ago. The people inhabiting them were close friends but alas, some of them are long gone from this earth.

Back in the 80's when we owned Olin Smith's Grocery Store; we came to know everyone within the area. We visited, delivered groceries to those unable to walk the short distance and it was lovely. The smiles from Mrs. Watkins, Mr. Ramey, Mrs. Sagely and others always filled the gloomiest of days. I never heard them complain as they were full of grace and thankfulness. Each of those houses, razed for a new King School addition, at one time held memories of families, growth and death. Where did all the memories go and are the spirits of those delightful people wondering the same thing?

One might ask me why I ask these questions but they are pertinent, especially when none of us know for certain where spirits go after death. If we can read and believe things through faith and have spiritual guidance, does it not stand to reason spirits do exist? Do spirits mingle or stay for prolonged periods of time after death, or are they mere figments of our imagination? Your guess is as good as mine but I do not want to push the envelope to find out. In due time, when it is time to reap rewards, I might find out. Until then, I will not speculate but know what I know.

Some things are not speculation as I will tell you. Before my mother passed away, I promised her I would make certain her house was thoroughly cleaned. Old things she and daddy accumulated piled in every corner of the house. It was not uncommon to find forty hairdryers, seventy five flashlights or bits and pieces of things they purchased at garage sales. Why they felt the need to bring home so many of those things is beyond me. I once told mother she only had one head and did not need another hairdryer. She laughed and told me the garage sale people needed the money. Daddy, on the other hand, felt the need to light up the world with flashlights. It was another one of his quirky collections. Anyway, as promised, I began cleaning the house. Daddy would only let me do so much as his penchant for keeping things kept me from tossing everything to the dump. It was a battle but did not come to war. He won and I resigned myself to let him enjoy whatever he wished.

About three weeks after mother passed away, daddy phoned me. He wanted to know if I had been at his house doing more cleaning. I told him no. When I asked him why, he told me I needed to see it to believe it. He was spooked! Now, daddy was not one to be frightened but this was one day I would see wide, steel grey eyes glaring back at me. As I pulled up to the house, daddy was sitting on the front porch. His words to me were, "Go in there and see if you see something strange." I went inside and burst into laughter.

Goosebumps shot up my spine. I told daddy it was mother sending a message. She would not hurt anyone but she was in a major snit. The living room had a large picture window facing the west with whatnot shelves around its perimeter. Old salt and pepper shakers we collected sat neatly in the nooks. A dining room table sat about four feet from the window. The curtain rod, with curtains attached, laid across the table. One of the last things mother told me was she hated the curtains and wanted something pretty on the curtain rod. Unfortunately, it was one of the things I had not done…get rid of those ugly curtains. Any way you slice it, mangle it or put it into a heap that curtain rod did not jump off the wall attachment and daddy did not take them down. He was not one to do housework of any kind. You can bet your bottom dollar, I did as mother requested and changed curtains that day!

I thought things had calmed down but not so. After daddy passed away, my sister Hazel and I began cleaning up the remaining clutter. We were in the bedroom looking at mother's clothing. As we piled good donating things to the side it was like we were intruding on mother's space. Both of us stopped dead in our tracks, laid down the clothes and walked to the front porch. We did not say one word to each other but nodded, as mother was saying it all.

You see, mother smoked Kool shorts, no filter and always used a sulfur match to light her cigarettes. It was ghastly in the house. Sulfur match scent was everywhere and it was so thick, you could not cut it with a knife. As we stood on the porch, it wafted around our heads. It was like mother was telling us our break was over; we needed to get back to work. Like two little kids, we obliged mother's wishes, ignored the sulfur scent but sure as heck would not forget the spirited gesture.

Even today, as Dan and I sit in our smoke free house, sulfur match scent drifts over our heads. We look at one another and nod. I am here to tell you, my mother's spirit is alive and well and I have other stories to match this one. Now, you tell me, where are those spirits and what are they doing on 20th Street?

THE THREE MONKEY MAXIM

Without a doubt, everyone reading this will have some type of what-not or do-dad in a nook of your house. Go ahead; I am not going anywhere so I will wait until you find that special object. Which one did you select? Does it remind you of a place, time or person? Can you hold it in your hand or clutch it near your heart? Collectables abound in every household whether they are large or small. They either belonged to someone you loved, given as a gift on a special occasion or found in an antique shop. It could be a delicate Faberge egg, your grandmother's butter churn or press, bisque china statues, jewelry, album, or as simple as a child's first birthday wax candle or tooth. Even reproductions of fine objet d'art can be sentimental. Things do not have to be expensive to be treasured.

My collections include a variety of things. Bells, chimes, old salt and pepper shakers, Indian arrowheads, marbles and a three monkey see no evil, hear no evil and speak no evil what-not. The little monkey maxim is not large nor is it worth much. It is another something to dust, hold in my hands and wonder about its origin. Mother had it long before I was born and I treasure it dearly. At one time each of the monkeys' had color. Blue for hear no evil, red for see no evil and green for speak no evil. Most of the color has worn away from years of touching but it still has meaning. Made of bisque it has Japan stamped on the back. If it had "occupied" Japan it might be of value. This tiny little object was used as a teaching tool when I was young. If I said something out of order Mother would cup her hands over my mouth. The same held true if I saw something I did not need to see or hear. She did not have to tell me why she was doing it as the three monkeys sat in plain view doing the same thing. Sometimes the colorful monkeys were a thorn in my side as they sat there with hands covering the most valuable tools of our being… mouth, eyes and ears. As a child, it was hard for me to keep my mouth, eyes and ears shut and even more so when three little monkeys dictated a powerful hand clamping gesture to me. If it was not Mother, it was those danged monkeys. At the time, I was in a no win situation but learned, as years went along, what those gestures meant.

A Picture Frame of Memories, Book I

It is hard to know the actual origin of the three monkeys but it is "folklore" in the Koshin belief. Based on Chinese Taoism, a Japanese monk, named Ennin, wrote a document in 838 A.D. when he visited China. Supposedly, this "folk religion" began with a thought that a person's body was inhabited by three worms. They were called Sanshi and kept tabs on a person's good and bad deeds if they saw, heard or spoke evil. During the Koshin wake, which occurs on every sixtieth day when a person is asleep, all of the Sanshi's (three worms) go to a heavenly God, (Ten-Tei), and report whether or not this person has done good or bad things. Many people thought they were made ill or would die because the Sanshi's reports to Ten-Tei. People tried to stay awake during the Koshin Machi (wake) to prevent terrible things from happening. The three worms, Sanshi, are believed to be related to the three monkeys, Mizaru (not see), Lwazaru (not say), and Kikazaru (not hear) because of the evil connotations of doing wrong. During the Edo era, the three monkeys were made into statues. They were regarded as Koshin keepers or guardians of a person's body from the evil "see, hear, say". Some Koshin monuments still standing in Japan today are made up of one, two or three monkeys of Japanese characters. A fourth monkey, (do no evil), is sometimes in current statuettes. Is all this fact or fiction?

I do not have a clue because I did not live in the year 838 A.D. and I am not privy to current Japanese comings, goings or folklore. When I was a kid, I did have a clue to know what Mother would do if I did not pay attention to her rules of the three monkey maxim. It did not hurt me to realize what I heard or saw should not be repeated. It would not serve a useful purpose to gossip about things that may or may not be true. Mother used to quote Abraham Lincoln as she pointed to the teaching tool. "Better to remain silent and be thought a fool than to speak out and remove all doubt."

The three monkeys tried to keep me in check but it did not always work. The solution that did work when I said something to Mother she did not like was made from a grungy old hog. The critters, namely the monkeys, may have been a teaching tool to help refine my better traits but the one critter, called hog lye soap, did more in one day than they did in a life time.

Hold your hand up if you had your mouth washed out with hog lard lye soap. I treasure my three little monkeys statuette but, by golly, I got even with the hog...I eat bacon!

THOSE WERE THE DAYS

Have you ever thought about all the things you have seen, used or did in your life time? How many things can you list that your child has never heard of or even knew existed? If you mention Lifebouy, would they think it is a life saving device? How about Fels-Naptha? Would your child even know how to use these products? If you mention Ajax, would they think it is a Trojan horse? What about Lux? If you told them you pulled a washcloth out of a Lux detergent box, would they believe you? If you mention McLean's, would they think of M*A*S*H* instead of toothpaste? If you said Tiger Paws® would they know you mean speeding like a tiger through hilly terrain with paws that grip…Uniroyal®? Would they believe you actually attached an artificial "tiger tails" to your gasoline cap? Would they understand "spin and twist to a forty-five" or would they think it is some kind of pistol?

What about carnival ware cup or saucer in a box of oats? How many of you collected them or did your mother shake the box to hear how hard it rattled? Was it a cup or saucer in that box? Kids would come unhinged if you found your old pair of blue suede loafers and did a quick b-bop to Elvis' old classic, Blue Suede Shoes. Leather penny loafers with Abraham Lincoln's face looking upward made girls blush. It was a rush to see how fast you could flip the penny over and shove it back inside the shoe before your face lost its glow. How many of us could wear a cinch belt...bet we don't have those twenty inch waists! Remember how we teased, prodded and wadded the hair for the beehive look? It couldn't be any worse than the razor sheared flat top. Even the pompadour made heads turn in disbelief. Sideburns swooped down the cheeks like hockey pucks and plucked eyebrows arched in menacing tones. Wearing DA's or DT's, aka duck tails, made parents drag kids to barbershops. Bright blue eye shadow glistened with glitter and inside the eye eyeliner made girls look like raccoons. False eyelashes came unglued and hung like tarantula legs on the nose. Everyone could tell you had false eyelashes on because they never were straight. Berets shaped like hearts would pop under the weight of hair and fling across the classroom. Stove leg jeans were made to make legs look like bird legs, the opposite of those were flares. Mention clam diggers with mesh stockings and three inch high heeled shoes. Scarves tied around the neck or ponytail served as a fashion accessory. The boys had a cigarette angled above the ear to look cool. How many of you had to sit in the principal's office for click-clacking taps down the hardwood floors? Shoving a stick of Blackjack chewing gum in the mouth to crack bubbles made parents climb walls.

Remember the fwap-fwap-fwap sound? Ah, come on. Anyone who had a bicycle, had to put baseball cards attached with clothespins on the wheel spokes. It was the sound you wanted to hear. It wasn't a loud muffler but you could mimic it. Drop a coin in the aperture, punch B-12 or your favorite selection and watch the forty-five slide from its slot and play those tunes. It was exciting to watch neon colored, flashing lights pulsate with the tempo on the Jukebox. Twirl the propeller, jazz it up with fishing lures or school slogans and you had a beanie. Red and blue…does it jiggle your sight? Made of cardboard, the lens on 3-D glasses tricked your brain into seeing a complete picture. Remember knock-knock jokes, mood rings, pet rocks, rubber band notes or eye-cat glasses?

Don't forget the chocolate! Those wanting to do something special for Valentine's Day always remember the bite and gag. It's a joke that is sometimes used on April fool's Day, too. Gather up wads of cotton, string, rubber bands or slender pieces of cardboard. Melt your delicious chocolate, carefully dip those individual items and cover them completely. The first bite, especially cotton, makes the teeth gritty. It is a shame to ruin chocolate but hysterically funny to watch someone spit, sputter and gag. Transistor radios were the thing to tote. Cramming kids into telephone booths and Volkswagens or climbing to the top of a flag pole was another craze. False beauty marks or wax moustaches, stuffing bras, mini or maxi skirts, raccoon caps…all at one time or another rattled our brains.

We've seen many presidents come and go, watched in horror of assassinations, viewed men as they walked on the moon, been in various wars, and were among the first to see a television. We saw the first computer and the stock market rise and crash, and we changed accordingly, as each decade brought new beginnings. There have been good things, bad things and everything in between. How sweet it is to know we have had so many opportunities to experience life in grace and crises and survive the odds to tell the tales.

As Edith and Archie Bunker of All in the Family would sing, "Those were the days!"

WOOLWORTHS & KRESS

The other day, while cleaning out cabinets to gut and re-do our kitchen, I came across a passel of recipes my mother collected. Anything mother collected is precious to me but like a lot of stuff, sometimes needs to be purged. Laying aside things I thought my children would enjoy, I thumbed through the pile of hand written notes. Some of the recipes were tattered and barely legible and others, well, they were concoctions my palate would not enjoy. I laid those in another pile to keep as a diet reminder. Then, the mother lode leapt into my hands. It nudged my memory like it was yesterday.

On occasion, if daddy had to work on Saturday, mother and I would walk seven blocks from our house to Main and Seventh Street. It always irked me that my sister was old enough to stay home because she did not want to "baby sit" someone five years younger than her, especially her sister. She had enough of babysitting when I was small and didn't want to put up with any more of my shenanigans. Climbing trees and catching bugs was not her forte. At the time, I did not realize I got the better deal of mother's plan. Right in front of Citizens Bank was an old, graying, slat back and seat, curled top bench with ornate metal arms and feet. We would sit there and wait until our ride ambled down the street.

It was an old Twin City bus shaped somewhat like a Quonset hut with an ugly flat face and horrible diesel exhaust. The bus stop, directly in front of Citizen's Bank, offered, for a small token, a scenic ride to Fort Smith. Swoosh, the door creaked open and we stepped upon a metal platform and then into the bus. We had to wait for the driver to collect our fare before we could sit on one of the seats. Mother always made me sit next to the window because she knew if I sat next to the narrow aisle, I would get up and talk to everyone on the bus. More than once, I tried to escape to the back of the "off limits" section to find out why they did not sit closer to the front of the bus.

Across the river we went, down Midland Boulevard to Fort Smith. It seemed like it took forever because the bus stopped at every other block to pick up riders or slammed on its brakes when someone pulled the dirty white cord at the top of the window. It made a buzzing sound indicating the rider needed to exit the bus. Finally, after jarring our innards with the thump of cobblestones beneath the wheels, we reached Fort Smith.

The town was magnificent with large buildings towering above my head, awnings in front of stores, listening to people talk and looking in storefronts of upscale fineries. One person I found fascinating was a gentleman, whose jovial disposition and pencil and razor blade selling technique, charmed me to the core. He was disabled in that his entire lower anatomy was amputated but it did not dissuade his desire to succeed. He managed to get around while sitting on a block of leather cushioned wood and using the same type of covered blocks for his hands. His hands were his feet. Even with his disability I never saw him without a smile on his face. If you bought his items, his slogan was 'Thanks if you do and thanks if you don't.' He was an inspiration.

Mother and I never went inside The Boston Store or Hunts Department Store but we did go to other delightful venues. Woolworths and Kress offered five and dime, a place most people could afford. Those two stores were packed with people perusing the latest stock or sitting at the counter waiting for a bite to eat. Kress offered hotdogs at a minimal price and fountain drinks. I do not think I have ever enjoyed a tastier hotdog or carbonated beverage in my life. Woolworth's offered other type of sandwiches, slices of layer cake, apple pie, shakes and banana splits. The highest priced sandwich was a chicken salad, three deck sandwich at sixty-five cents. I remember watching them place bacon on a grill and using a hot coffee pot to mash the bacon flat. The BLT was another three deck sandwich for fifty cents. They always featured Coca Cola.

What mother ordered was a two slice, toasted ham salad sandwich for thirty cents although it could be ordered as three deck. I remember her counting her change to make sure she had enough money. She and I would sit on the red, plastic covered, twirling bar stools and all I wanted to do was whirl it around in circles. I am sure I pushed her to the limits in patience. The sandwich mother ordered was always cut into three sections. She ate one small portion and I ate another. The third portion mother wrapped inside a paper napkin and we brought it home. At the time, I supposed it was for my sister but when I saw mother dissecting the sandwich, I realized it was for other purposes. She wanted to find out the ingredients so she could make it at home without going to Fort Smith.

The mother lode of my recipe find was for ham salad. At the top of the page it titled "Woolworth's

Ham Salad Sandwich." I do not know if this is the correct ingredients but here is what mother deciphered from taking the sandwich apart.

Baked ham, diced. Finely chopped celery. Sweet pickle relish, however much you like to taste. Enough Miracle Whip for consistency (she never used mayo as it was too expensive). Salt and fresh ground pepper. Four slices whole wheat bread toasted. Two lettuce leaves. Her note said to dice the ham (do not mince or grind) and add diced celery, sweet pickle relish, salt and pepper to taste and salad dressing to form a nice spread. Put on toasted bread, top with a lettuce leaf and continue until you have a three deck sandwich.

Without question, I got the better deal made from memories and recipes!

MATLOCK'S GROCERY STORE

At the Rotary Club where I spoke, someone asked if I knew Guy and Jewell Matlock. My answer was yes that I had mentioned them in one of my stories. If you grew up in the hollers, everyone knew these wonderful people. Even if you didn't, some of you might have visited their quaint little grocery store. In the beginning, their grocery store was on the east side of Lafayette Street, just three or four houses away from the corner of Cedar and Lafayette Streets. When I was growing up, Cedar Street in the hollers was called Clay Street. I don't know if it was because the soil was comprised of the icky goop or the city didn't have a better name for it. Later, a sign popped up and we had to call it Cedar Street.

Matlock's Grocery Store had a small dirt parking lot and it was always full of cars. If it was not cars congregating in the parking lot, it was kids. People would run in there for bread, milk or lunch meats. Inside the store, the counter was immediately to the left. All kinds of penny candy lay beneath the counter inside a glass case. To its right was a large, red chest

Coke machine. Raising the heavy lid, bottled cokes sat neatly in rows beneath a sliding rim. In order to retrieve your favorite drink, a dime (went up from a nickel) had to be inserted into a narrow aperture and a coke would slide gently out of its slot. The cokes nestled inside crystal clear small chunks of ice keeping them cold. Angled beneath the ice were varieties of other liquid beverages. Nesbitt's orange and grape colas, Royal Crown Cola, root beer, Ginger ale, Pepsi and chocolate drinks. In the summer we would raise the soft drink lid to feel a soothing cool blast to ease a weary hot face or snatch a chunk of ice for a temporary taste of liquid.

Their small store was not like stores of today. The building did not go on forever in every which cockeyed direction and the isles did not have cart to cart collisions. Cereal aisles were calm with two or three different varieties. It was Post Toasties, Rice Krispies, Corn Flakes, Wheaties, Grape Nuts and maybe an odd whatever thrown in for good measure. Quaker Oats, Malt-O- Meal and Nabisco Cream of Wheat was the choice of hot breakfast meals.

Canned good aisles did not boast forty-eleven brands and there were not baked beans with a price soaring to $2.06 per can that I saw in a super center the other day. Ghastly and unconscionable! Most canned good prices ranged from fifteen to twenty-five cents per can. It was green beans, pork and beans, corn, hominy, whole tomatoes and a few other selections…with most of them under the same brand. There was not a sea of white labels announcing a store's private label.

You did not see tomato paste, puree, sauce, or chunks, diced, or spiced. Nearly every can of what you purchased was sixteen ounces, like it or leave it. If you wanted to eat some type of bean you purchase a bag of dried peas or beans. No ethnic foods dotted the shelves. The choice of lunch meats included rolls of bologna, pickle loaf, liver loaf and hogs head cheese. Cheddar cheese came in big slabs with red waxy exteriors. Swiss cheese was an option. Limburger, a stinky obnoxious cheese, was there for those who could stomach its taste and could live to tell about it. Each of these meats and cheeses were sliced as they did not come in individual packages. Bread was either Holsum or Colonial. Tuna was packed in oil and sardines came in mustard sauce. They had everyday staples such as milk, eggs, bacon and lard and vegetables and fruits. It was an all 'round friendly neighborhood grocery store.

The Matlock's were great people and treated everyone with respect. They had a running tab for most people and knew the people would pay what they owed. It was like an old fashioned handshake...your hand was your bond.

Guy and Jewell's living quarters was connected to the store. Some mornings if you needed something in a hurry before store hours, all you had to do was knock. Jewell or Guy would unlock the door to let you purchase what you needed. It was not uncommon for Jewell to greet you in her house robe and curlers in her hair. As their business grew, they moved to the west corner of Lafayette and Franklin Streets. It was at the opposite end of the block near Mt. Olive Methodist Church. It was a white concrete block building and the atmosphere of their business stayed the same...warm and inviting. Again, their living quarters was connected to the store.

There are so many people I remember seeing in Matlock's Grocery Store. The store was alive with different personalities and all of them lived within walking distance to the store. Families, living in the holler and surrounding area, needed the convenient little grocery store and it would not have happened without Guy and Jewell Matlock.

Occasionally I will drive Lafayette Street. Some changes to my old stomping grounds have been good. A new apartment complex has been erected where Matlock's second grocery store used to be. The rest of the street seems to be hinged in the 50's.

However good, bad, old or new…I smile because I see ghosts of yesteryear waving at me…and I wave back.

Footnote:

When I e-mailed Bill Matlock to get permission to use his parent's name / business in this book, he e-mailed me back. His words to me were precious.

You have been given a great gift of communicating through the written word. You have a style of writing that draws people back to their youth, opens a window of memories that has been closed too long. Your words open that window and bring a fresh breeze of fond memories from the past. You have the ability to bring a smile or a chuckle from your stories but there is a deeper response that makes your writings special. They make the reader realize that the foundation of experiences and memories from their past actually make up much of whom they have become.

I know just before you go on stage for a performance there is an old sayings "break a leg." I'm not sure what you say to a gifted writer about to feature her next book so I will just paraphrase by saying "break a pencil."

Please let me know what your publish dates will be…looking forward to reading your books.

As Bob Hope use to say "Thanks for the Memories"

Bill Matlock

DOG DAYS

As far back as I can remember, the terms "it's the dogs", Dog Days or "dog days of summer", have been bandied about with rancor. Adults sang the same tune but never a complete stanza. When I was small, I didn't have a clue what the hullabaloo was all about, but take it from me; I wondered if dogs had a special day set aside to coincide with summer. I expected to see a pack of dogs running down the street or a few howling at the moon. When daddy let out a few "damn dog days" while attacking grasshoppers perched on the windshield wipers, I was thoroughly confused. A few days later, wasps and other stinging insects felt his wrath. Just what the heck were dog days, and why, if it was for the dogs were grasshoppers and other objects of disdain being targeted? The confusion intensified as he was rubbing his feet spewing forth, "My dogs are tired because of the dog days."

Mother appeared exhausted as I watched her wipe her brow with a cool cloth. She always wore dresses (it was unheard of women wearing slacks) and occasionally, I would see her sway the hem of her dress to catch a breeze. Collapsing in a chair, she'd let out a "momma sigh", (the kind of air escaping when a woman is fed up--yeah, the women know what it is), and she'd blister the air with a few choice words always ending with dog days. I thought, poor old dogs best be staying away from our household or they might be fodder for the hogs.

The song didn't end with Mother and Daddy. By gum, all the adults in the neighborhood must have known the same tune because the spirited gift hinged from their mouths, too. It was the weirdest thing ever to hit Henry Street. A plague especially designed for the adults. Funny thing, all the kids thought it was a sinister disease projected from a hydrophobic dog. We never did see any dogs but they were being cursed like the devil.

All the time I was growing up, if I didn't know how to spell or pronounce a word, Daddy would yell, "Look it up in the dictionary." How in thunder was I supposed to look up any word if it contained zeds in multiple quads? Lucky me, I learned to spell at an early age and used Webster more often than there are legs in a centipede convoy. I flipped through the C & D, black thumb index and found my answer. At long last, Dog Days came alive through more searches in words describing the heinous little bright star. I was not in to astronomy other than the North Star and Milky Way and knew nothing relative to its history.

Sirius, the Dog Star, is the culprit. He rises and sets with the sun and is also the brightest star, besides the Sun. People used to believe it was an evil time, according to Brady's, *Clavis Calendarium,* 1813, "when the seas boiled, wine turned sour, dogs grew mad, and all creatures became languid, causing to man burning fevers, hysterics, and phrensies." The Old Farmer's Almanac "dog days of summer" usually begins in the latter part of July and continues through to the middle of August. Sweltering heat pounds the earth with gusto as the sun is directly above us during this period. I don't know how many of you watch the sun as it proceeds in seasonal changes. During the delightful spring and fall evenings, my husband, Dan, and I watch the sun set while we sit on our back porch. It is a remarkable site to know our earth's revolution is so slow, you can actually watch it in action. During its cycle, a person can tell when the months are changing. It takes six months for the sun to go from the south to north (December to June) and six months (June to December) in the opposite direction, making up one full year. For those of you who have a computer, look up this source as it explains in detail what my husband and I see when we watch the sun.

It may be hard to believe a single Dog Star, millions of miles away from earth, could work in conjunction with the Sun to create the atmospheric phenomenon searing our little corner of the world, but it does. At this point in my life, having experiencing the dreaded Dog Days, I can understand why my parents and other adults were going ballistic. Strange isn't it, I learned the lyrics to their song and the stanza always ends with "damned dog days." The heat feels like it is at a boiling point, triggering tempers and putting the body in slow motion. Just like it was when I was a child, it is today, the dog days of summer continue.

It does appear as the old saying goes ... "The more that things do change, the more they stay the same" because "nothing is new under the sun."

Source: http://en.wikipedia.org/wiki/Dog_Days
Source: http://en.wikipedia.org/wiki/Solstice

SATURDAY SHOPPING & TRIANGLE

Saturday was a busy day in the lives of those who operated downtown stores. It started early at 8 am with shoppers eager to find the latest fashion at Hay's and Graham, W.B. Smith Dry Goods Store, Mode O'Day or Comstock's. A lot of shoppers placed their selection on credit but not with plastic cards. The proprietors rang up sales, wrote down what you purchased on fold over ledgers and put them in card files. It was done on the trust factor as they knew you were good for those purchases. Some purchases were on THT, take home for trial to see if it fit. If it did not fit, you returned it unsoiled, no questions asked.

Southern Café, where my Grandma Hawkins worked as a cook, was right next door to the Cottage Café, well known for special pies. Both cafes were extraordinary as the mouth-watering food and aromas filled every nook and cranny of downtown. They drew you in like a magnet. A small entryway, next to the Southern Café, housed a staircase leading to Dr. Patton's office. He was a general practitioner. Since he had many patients, he kept the drug stores busy filling prescriptions.

Hardware stores, dotting the main drag, were equally as busy plying all those needing some type of tool to sitting around chewing the fat. Van Buren Feed Store and the Farmers Cooperative saw tons of shoppers needing to refill the larder for livestock. Three barber shops, two on Main Street and the other on Seventh Street, had men waiting for their turn for a shave and hair cut … six bits, while the beauty shops were overrun by women wanting the latest coif.

Twenty dollars would allow for four big paper sacks full of groceries and two bags of non essentials. Meat markets cut their own meats and displayed them in glass cases and would wrap your choice of cuts in butcher paper tied with string. If you had other shopping to do, they were happy to hold your purchase to keep it from spoiling.

For some, it was not all work and no play. Some men dropped in for a game of snooker or cards at Fisher's Pool Hall / Parlor. Many people could not resist the delightful doughnut shop near the parlor. While parents did shopping, the kids were eager to go to the Bob Burn's Theater. It was their home away from home on those, "I do not want to go shopping" days. Parents did not have to worry about their children or what they were doing.

The citizens of Van Buren totaled roughly six thousand and everyone knew one another by first name. Most often it was because relatives were plenty, either by blood kin or cousins six or seven times down the family tree. You could rest assured, most everyone knew what kid belonged to what parent, and they did not hesitate to let a parent know when a child was out of line. It was like a large extended family, kin or not, without paying someone else's taxes.

No one complained about trekking up and down Main Street or for waiting on a parking spot to be available. Most times, the town would be so full of vehicles, it was bumper to bumper. No one could speed up and down the street because of the cobblestone pavement. It sounded like thunder inside the car and shook the innards like a milkshake. Although the cobblestone needed repairs when a cobble jutted into the air, it gave the town character. It was a quaint atmosphere showing off its grandeur in an ageless time capsule. I found it sad when asphalt covered those impressive, beautiful cobbles. It turned the town into a sophisticated state but took away the laid by hand beauty.

To have our town labeled as a true historic downtown, the cobblestones of Van Buren need to be uncovered. There were no parking meters or stop lights and drivers were accommodating to those needing to turn onto Main Street. It was reciprocity. There was no fear of retaliation as road hogs did not exist. On occasion, there were fender benders but a handshake usually took care of the promise to mend dents. Road rage was not a factor because a man's word and handshake was his bond. Just about everyone used the same insurance agent whose location was on the main drag. If there was a dispute, the insurance agent mediated and settled the problem.

At the time, the excursion train did not exist but the Frisco trains did their part to backlog traffic on Log Town hill. At the time, the Frisco railroad provided passenger trains for those needing to travel north toward Fayetteville and beyond. People wanting to exit onto Knox Street squeezed perilously close to the train to avoid waiting for the train to move on down the rail.

Do you remember the triangle? It was where patrons went after the usual Saturday foray into town. The triangle was a necessary last stop as businesses were closed on Sunday (Blue Law next story). How they crammed so many things in one spot was amazing. At the top of Main Street where Sharon's Dog Grooming is located, there was a hubbub of activity.

It was Carl Sullivan's Skelly station providing many customers a place for their automobiles to be repaired and gasoline. Although it was a small area, Mr. Sullivan managed to service cars, pump gasoline for customers and do it all with a smile. Right in front of his store was a narrow street. It was a continuation of Webster Street coming up the slight hill from the post office. Directly across the street, on the north side of Webster was Coble's Conoco, two pump, gasoline station. Access to Coble's, via a quick turn, was either from Main Street or a whip through from Webster. Gasoline, pumped by these two fine gentlemen, was around twenty cents a gallon.

Where there was a will, there was a way. Where there was a need you didn't have to look too far to find the solution. Everything, along with the triangle and twenty cents a gallon gasoline is gone as time marks its season with every revolution.

Joyce L. Rapier

COUNTRY LIVING & DIRT ROADS

True country living, some forty-plus years ago, was pristine, serene, beautiful and captivating. Its dusty roads, sometimes leading to nowhere, gave way to adventure as I wondered where they would take us as we ventured further through the tree lined archways. Off the side of the roads, massive oak branches entwined with wild muscadine vines, blackberry thorns and an occasional Creeping Charley. It indicated footsteps did not trod through those precious fauna and over grown woodlands. It was as though time was standing still to be the way it was hundreds of years ago when nature ruled the forests. Springtime in the mountains showed its beauty with blooming Dogwood trees, wild Plum and wild honeysuckle. An occasional squirrel could be seen sunning itself on a fork in the tree. Sometimes a snake would be slithering across the road or curled upon a rock. Deer was present but not seen as they are smarter than humans and knew when to hide. Nature's camouflage hides a multitude of things we wish we could see, and maybe, sometimes, it's a good thing we can't see it.

Bumpy roads, with boulders as large as the eye could see, hinged together as one, unifying a kindred spirit. A cornucopia of moss and ferns wedged inside crevices of rock pillars and jutting, ragged edges of mountain terrain was a perfect picture of harmony. Nothing could be more magnificent than viewing the world from the crest of a winding dirt road. Breathtaking, untouched vistas had a way of garnering attention, whether by a person out for a Sunday drive or those wanting to partake of its newfound building sites.

Often, on our autumn journey to the country to view the remarkable hues of red, yellow and orange trees, we would stop at a safe area and peer over the cliffs. A chimney, down in a small valley, would be puffing light gray smoke. I wondered how many of its residents were sitting by the fireside wrapped up inside a cozy blanket or what was cooking on the stove. The scent of hickory wood mixed with the faint aroma of bacon and eggs or pinto beans cooking tempted a knock on the door. Alas, we ventured on our way with unanswered questions.

Dirt roads have character. Not because they are dusty or bumpy but because it is a creation, of sorts, in attitude. People living in the country aren't cumbered by what their neighbors think, what kind of vehicle they need to drive or such. The kids are beautiful as they can find things to do without sitting in front of a computer or surfing TV channels to keep them occupied. They are happy, robust children because of country living. Every time we saw children playing, they were laughing or smiling and waved, letting us know it was their way of saying hello. Fishing poles were slung across the shoulder and sometimes a passel of fish dangled from a string indicating a day of sitting on a creek bank was worthwhile. People in the country are not idle folks. The majority of them have gardens to work, cows and livestock to tend and /or a tedious nine to five job in the city. It is a way of life.

I suppose my fondness for country living and the quiet atmosphere came from an overnight stay with a friend. It was the first time I had been invited to stay overnight in the country with a school mate. Sue lived a few miles down the country road by the old school house in Figure Five. Going toward Cedar Creek, the road was narrow in spots, but who was going to argue with a massive, bright yellow school bus? Although the bus was loud with boys and girls laughter, and the exhaust fumes were somewhat overwhelming at successive drop off points, I couldn't wait to get to her house. As the cumbersome bus ambled down the road I was in awe. When we stepped from the bus, I got lumps in my throat. Not from fear but excitability.

Sue's house, perched on the side of small knoll, was, in my opinion, perfect. Her parents were lovely and I felt at home. It was genuine, southern hospitality. Although I cannot remember what we had for supper, the wood stove exuded a delightful aroma. Going outside, the fresh air with an occasional whiff of hickory keyed and enhanced the countryside. An indelible impression wrapped around me as I walked through sweet grass, listened to crickets chirp, and heard songs on the wind from croaking frogs. When it was time for bed and lights went out, I was charmed with the feather mattress. Soft and cozy, I could feel my body melt into the warmth of its surround, and the homemade quilts piled atop us added to the comfort. All too soon, the overnight stay was over. Just as the sun was breaking through the trees, it was time to greet the bus driver for another day of school.

Now, many years later from the overnight stay, dirt roads and quiet country existence are becoming a thing of the past. Asphalt is, bit by bit, creeping into the quite repose and replacing quaint country living with fast paced, clock ticking lifestyles. Houses are larger than ever displacing those small houses I came to enjoy, and there are no dirt roads with children in search of a fishing hole or little girls waving hello.

Some people will never see a dirt road, enjoy a quiet ride in the country or capture the essence of natural beauty. Country living and dirt roads, as I once knew it, are now, alas ... suburbia.

A Picture Frame of Memories, Book I

I do hope you enjoyed reading these stories as much as I loved writing them. These are but a few of my favorite things and memories and the second book, ***Skipping Down Memory Lane***, will be coming in short order.

-Joyce

Made in the USA
Charleston, SC
16 March 2011